2004

PLATO'S
Symposium

OXFORD APPROACHES TO

CLASSICAL LITERATURE

SERIES EDITORS
Kathleen Coleman and Richard Rutherford

OVID'S *Metamorphoses*
ELAINE FANTHAM

PLATO'S *Symposium*
RICHARD HUNTER

PLATO'S
Symposium

RICHARD HUNTER

UNIVERSITY PRESS

2004

OXFORD
UNIVERSITY PRESS

Oxford   New York

Auckland   Bangkok   Buenos Aires   Cape Town   Chennai
Dar es Salaam   Delhi   Hong Kong   Istanbul   Karachi   Kolkata
Kuala Lumpur   Madrid   Melbourne   Mexico City   Mumbai   Nairobi
São Paulo   Shanghai   Taipei   Tokyo   Toronto

Copyright © 2004 by Oxford University Press, Inc.

Published by Oxford University Press, Inc.
198 Madison Avenue, New York, New York 10016

www.oup.com

Oxford is a registered trademark of Oxford University Press

Library of Congress Cataloging-in-Publication Data
Hunter, R. L. (Richard L.)
Plato's Symposium / Richard Hunter.
p. cm. — (Oxford approaches to classical literature)
Includes bibliographical references and index.
ISBN 0-19-516079-7; 0-19-516080-0 (pbk.)
1. Plato. Symposium.   I. Title.   II. Series.
B385.H85   2004
184—dc22   2004004566

1   3   5   7   9   8   6   4   2

Printed in the United States of America
on acid-free paper

Editors' Foreword

The late twentieth and early twenty-first centuries have seen a massive expansion in courses dealing with ancient civilization and, in particular, the culture and literature of the Greek and Roman world. Never has there been such a flood of good translations available: Oxford's own World Classics, the Penguin Classics, the Hackett Library, and other series offer the English-speaking reader access to the masterpieces of classical literature from Homer to Augustine. The reader may, however, need more guidance in the interpretation and understanding of these works than can usually be provided in the relatively short introduction that prefaces a work in translation. There is a need for studies of individual works that will provide a clear, lively, and reliable account based on the most up-to-date scholarship without dwelling on minutiae that are likely to distract or confuse the reader.

It is to meet this need that the present series has been devised. The title *Oxford Approaches to Classical Literature* deliberately puts the emphasis on the literary works themselves. The volumes in this series will each be concerned with a single work (with the exception of cases where a "book" or larger collection of poems is treated as one work). These are neither biographies nor accounts of literary movements or schools. Nor are they books devoted to the total oeuvre of one author: our first volumes consider Ovid's *Metamorphoses* and Plato's *Symposium*, not the works of Ovid or Plato as a whole. This is, however, a question of emphasis, and not a straitjacket: biographical issues, literary and cultural background, and related works by the same author are discussed where they are obviously relevant. The series' authors have also been encouraged to consider the influence and legacy of the works in question.

As the editors of this series, we intend these volumes to be accessible to the reader who is encountering the relevant work for the first time; but we also intend that each volume should do more than simply provide the basic facts, dates, and summaries that handbooks generally supply. We would like these books to be essays in criticism and interpretation that will do justice to the subtlety and complexity of the works under discussion. With this in mind, we have invited leading scholars to offer personal assessments and appreciation of their chosen works, anchored within the mainstream of classical scholarship. We have thought it particularly important that our authors be allowed to set their own agendas and to speak in their own voices rather than repeating the *idées reçues* of conventional wisdom in neutral tones.

The title *Oxford Approaches to Classical Literature* has been chosen simply because the series is published by Oxford University Press, USA; it in no way implies a party line, either Oxonian or any other. We believe that different approaches are suited to different texts, and we expect each volume to have its own distinctive character. Advanced critical theory is neither compulsory nor excluded: what matters is whether it can be made to illuminate the text in question. The authors have been encouraged to avoid obscurity and jargon, bearing in mind the needs of the general reader; but, when important critical or narratological issues arise, they are presented to the reader as lucidly as possible.

This series was originally conceived by Professor Charles Segal, an inspiring scholar and teacher whose intellectual energy and range of interests were matched by a corresponding humility and generosity of spirit. Although he was involved in the commissioning of a number of volumes, he did not—alas—live to see any of them published. The series is intended to convey something of the excitement and pleasure to be derived from reading the extraordinarily rich and varied literature of Greco-Roman antiquity. We hope that these volumes will form a worthy monument to a dedicated classical scholar who was committed to enabling the ancient texts to speak to the widest possible audience in the contemporary world.

Kathleen Coleman, Harvard University
Richard Rutherford, Christ Church, Oxford

Preface

This volume is an introductory and explanatory study of the *Symposium*. I hope that it will be found useful by those who have already read or are in the process of reading the *Symposium*; my most fervent hope, however, is to persuade those who fall into neither category that they should become acquainted with Plato's marvelous work without delay.

I am very much indebted to the encouragement and advice of the general editors of this new series, Kathleen Coleman and Richard Rutherford. Earlier versions of the entire typescript were also read by Nicholas Denyer, Demetra Koukouzika, Frisbee Sheffield, and Anthony Verity; all saved me from error and pointed me in fruitful directions. I am very grateful to them.

When I first accepted an invitation to contribute to this series, one of the general editors was Charles Segal. It is a matter of great sadness to me that I was unable to benefit from his criticism. I have no idea what he would have thought of this little book, but it is nevertheless dedicated to the memory of this extraordinary scholar: no one did more to show why classical literature still matters, and there are very few works that still matter more than Plato's *Symposium*.

Contents

Editors' Foreword   *v*

Preliminary Note   *xiii*

1

Setting the Scene   *3*

2

Erôs before Socrates   *38*

3

The Love of Socrates   *78*

4

The Morning After   *113*

Bibliography and Further Reading   *137*

Index of Passages Discussed   *145*

General Index   *147*

Preliminary Note

Translations from the *Symposium* which are set off from the main body of the text are taken from Plato, *Symposium*, translated by Robin Waterfield (Oxford 1994). In-text translations are usually my own. Where not otherwise acknowledged, all translations from other Greek and Latin works are my own.

PLATO'S
Symposium

·1·

Setting the Scene

1 | Symposia and *Symposium*

Plato's *Symposium* is the account of a (presumably fictional) gathering in the house of the Athenian tragic poet Agathon to celebrate his first victory in 416 BC in one of the great dramatic festivals of the city;[1] the work itself was probably composed in the period 385–370 BC, and belongs to the same broad period as some of Plato's other most famous works, such as *Phaedo, Phaedrus,* and *Republic.*[2] The *Symposium* looks back to a remarkable period in Athenian history, shortly before the city undertook a major military expedition to Sicily which was to end in disaster and which, at least with hindsight, could be seen to have ushered in the era which culminated in

---

[1] The date presumably goes back ultimately to official Athenian records. Our source for the date (Athenaeus, *Deipnosophistai* 5.217a) records that the victory was at the Lenaian festival, but Plato magnifies the occasion by a number of suggestions of the more glorious Great Dionysia; cf. Sider (1980).

[2] For more detailed discussion of the date of composition of the *Symposium,* cf. Mattingly (1958) and Dover (1965). Scholarly consensus makes Xenophon's *Symposium* imitate Plato, not vice versa; cf. Huss (1999) 13–25.

catastrophic Athenian defeat in the Peloponnesian War (404 BC); as we shall see, Plato in various ways foreshadows the storm which would a year later engulf some of Agathon's most prominent guests. The story is narrated by one Apollodorus, a follower of Socrates, to a group of acquaintances, apparently "wealthy business men" (173c6); Apollodorus's source for his account is another follower of Socrates, Aristodemus, who had been present himself at Agathon's symposium. When the conversation between Apollodorus and the anonymous acquaintances is imagined to have taken place is left somewhat hazy. Socrates is still alive (he was executed in 399), but the symposium was clearly some time ago (173a5), and Agathon has not lived in Athens "for many years" (172c3); the poet is usually thought to have left Athens for the court of Archelaos of Macedon in or close to 408. We are clearly then at the very end of the fifth century.

The final part of the *Symposium* is illuminated by the brilliant figure of Alcibiades, who dominated Athenian political life in the closing years of the Peloponnesian War.[3] Coming from the highest and richest echelons of Athenian society, Alcibiades, who would probably have been in his early thirties at the dramatic date of the *Symposium*, used his social and rhetorical power to persuade the Athenians to undertake the expedition to Sicily and to have himself elected as one of its generals. Summoned back from the expedition to answer charges of profaning the Eleusinian Mysteries (see p. 14), he escaped to Sparta where he did signal service for Athens's enemies. More than once the Athenians recalled him, but the relationship between the democracy and its most wayward son was never to be an easy one; there can be little doubt that Socrates' association with such a man counted against him at the philosopher's trial in 399. Alcibiades was murdered in Asia Minor in 404, and a setting for the *Symposium* shortly before then, when there was intense Athenian interest in his intentions (perhaps dramatized in the *Symposium*'s opening frame), or just after would make good sense. There is in fact no compelling reason to think of Alcibiades as still alive at

[3] For Alcibiades cf. Gribble (1999) and Nails (2002) 10–20, both with earlier bibliography.

the dramatic time of the fictional conversation, and death is a very powerful provocation to anecdotal memory.

The *symposium* (drinking together) in private houses is one of the most familiar features of the male social culture of archaic and classical Greece. After the part of the gathering principally devoted to eating, guests would wash and pour libations to the "Agathos Daimon" (Divinity of Good Fortune) and to "Zeus the Savior" (cf. 176a); the host or a "ruler of the symposium" chosen by the guests (*symposiarchos*; cf. 213e9; Plutarch, *Sympotic Questions* 1.4) would then decide how much wine was to be drunk and in what strength— Greeks drank their wine heavily (by our standards) diluted with water. Agathon's guests come to a mutual and "democratic"[4] decision that no one is to be compelled to drink anything (176b–e)— "good order" (*kosmos*) is to be a watchword of this party, at least until Alcibiades enters and, in a jestingly autocratic spirit, but one appropriate to someone whose excesses were thought to suggest designs on tyranny,[5] elects himself symposiarch (213e9). As the "father of the *logos*" (177d5), that is, the person responsible for suggesting the subject of the speeches, Phaedrus takes some of the role of symposiarch (cf. 194d, 199b6–c2), and Eryximachus too helps to keep the company to their agreed scheme of encomia, but mutuality is a hallmark of the self-effacing Agathon's guests. The newly arrived Alcibiades, however, already "very drunk" (212d4), seeks to impose a new order of hard drinking (214a–b), and this is one of the ways in which his entry will mark a new start for the symposium (see p. 98).

Another crucial decision for the conduct of the symposium was how the guests were to pass the time and what entertainment was to be offered. Conversation, music (176e7), games, and sexual banter were, along with wine, the basic material of any symposium. One common form of sympotic verbal game, the "likeness"—"Why is X (usually one of the symposiasts) like Y (usually something non-human)?"—is played out in Alcibiades' description of Socrates as a

[4] Eryximachus's language at 176e4–5—"now that this has been agreed . . ."— may perhaps gesture to the language of public decrees.

[5] Thucydides 6.15.4; Plutarch, *Alcibiades* 16.2, 5.

carved Silenus. The performance and discussion of poetry, whether by a recognized poet or by the guests themselves (each often required to cap the preceding presentation), were also standard features of such gatherings.[6] Agathon's performance (cf. below, pp. 71–77) and Alcibiades' "satyric drama" (cf. below, pp. 98–112) are the principal "poetic" offerings with which Plato entertains *his* guests/readers, though the other performers also liberally sprinkle their speeches with references to and quotations from the poets. In Plato's day the recitation of famous speeches from Attic drama would have been a standard sympotic entertainment.

The symposium was an "alternative society," conducted by its own rules and rituals, which both reflected upon and often inverted the conventions of ordinary society; within the sealed space of male exchange and under the liberating influence of Dionysus and his wine, many of the conventional constraints imposed by the public gaze could be relaxed and festive license given free rein. The alterity of sympotic space will be a crucial factor in many of the speeches we will hear. Moreover, from the very earliest period the conduct of the symposium itself is an important topic of sympotic literature; the overriding interest in their own procedures which characterizes the members of many modern clubs and societies found an ancient counterpart in sympotic reflections upon symposia. Plato's *Symposium* is to be seen within an evolving fourth-century tradition of prose *sympotika*, which develop the themes of the sympotic poetry of the earlier archaic period.[7] One of the most famous of such idealizing reflections upon behavior at the symposium is from Xenophanes of Colophon (second half of sixth–early fifth century):

For now the floor is clean and clean the hands of everyone and the cups; [one servant] places woven garlands round [the heads of the guests], and another offers sweet-smelling per-

[6] Helpful surveys and further bibliography are in Stehle (1997) chapter 5 and Ford (2002) chapter 1.

[7] In addition to Xenophon's *Symposium*, important parts of the *Cyropaideia* are also relevant; note also Plato, *Protagoras* 347c–e, *Laws* books 1–2; Tecusan (1990). The standard treatment of the symposium in literature is Martin (1931).

fume in a saucer; the mixing-bowl stands filled with good cheer; on hand is additional wine, which promises never to run out, mellow in its jars and fragrant with its bouquet; in the middle incense sends forth its pure and holy aroma and there is water, cool, sweet, and clear; nearby are set golden-brown loaves and a magnificent table laden with cheese and thick honey; in the centre an altar is covered all over with flowers, and song and festivity pervade the room.

For men of good cheer should first hymn the god with reverent tales and pure words, after pouring libations and praying for the ability to do what is right (*dikaia*) . . . not commit deeds of violence (*hybreis*); one should drink as much as you can hold and come home without any attendant unless you are very old, and praise that man who after drinking reveals noble thoughts, so that there is a recollection and striving for excellence (*aretê*); one should not recount the battles of the Titans or Giants or Centaurs, creations of our predecessors, or violent factions—there is nothing useful in them; and one should always have a good regard for the gods. (Xenophanes fr. 1; trans. Gerber, adapted)

The composition of such a poem is a highly elite activity, characteristic of a socially and politically privileged group. There has been much debate as to how elite an institution the Athenian symposium itself, which presumably existed in many different degrees of formality, was felt to be, at least by the late fifth century (or indeed the time of Plato).[8] Broadly speaking, Plato's *Symposium* depicts a well-to-do, elite class, such as indeed seems to have been Socrates' regular circle, and it is likely enough that such ritualized and rather self-conscious symposia, as opposed to less-formal communal drinking, could indeed be felt to be an institution of the "upper classes," rather remote from the practical concerns and limited time and domestic space available to ordinary, working people. Socrates both is, and is not, part of that elite.

[8] The debate may be tracked through Murray (1990b); Bowie (1997) 3; Fisher (2000); Wilkins (2000) 202–11.

Modern historians of the symposium rightly distinguish the feasting and entertainment of Homeric banquets from the archaic and classical symposium, where for example the guests reclined on shared couches rather than, as in Homer, sitting alone. Nevertheless, it was principally the hospitality described in the *Odyssey* (Nestor at Pylos, Menelaus at Sparta, Alcinous on Scheria) which provided the authorizing Homeric pattern after which post-Homeric symposiasts could model themselves, just as the Cyclops and Penelope's suitors provided the antimodel to be avoided. Odysseus's "golden verses" offer the ideal:

> It is a lovely thing to listen to a bard such as this whose voice resembles that of the gods. Indeed, I think that there is nothing more delightful (lit. having more *charis*) than when festivity (*euphrosynê*) reigns over all the people, the banqueters in the palace sit in orderly sequence and listen to the bard, the tables near by are laden with bread and meat, and the wine-pourer draws wine from the mixing-bowl and pours it into the cups. This seems to me the very loveliest thing. (Homer, *Odyssey* 9.3–11)

So too, the Olympian feast of the gods highlights laughter and Apolline music, even though divisive strife is never far away (cf. *Iliad* 1.571–611). Among Demodocus's songs to the feasting Phaeacians in *Odyssey* 8, it is the story of Hephaestus catching Ares in bed with his wife, Aphrodite, which is most important for the later symposium. Hephaestus traps the lovers with invisible chains spread over his wife's bed and then summons the other gods to witness the couple's shame. This "naughty" cautionary tale of desire, clearly designed for a male audience (cf. vv. 367–69), itself orchestrates the response of laughter (vv. 326, 343) and pleasure (v. 368) which is appropriate to the symposium, and which also greets Alcibiades' account of his "sexual relations" with Socrates (222c1). There is not a little in common between the story of Ares and Aphrodite, bound fast in bed by Hephaestus's magic chains in a fate which both Apollo and Hermes would give anything to enjoy (*Odyssey* 8.321–43), and Aristophanes' tale in the

Symposium of how Hephaestus offers to weld a happy couple together so that their two bodies are fused into one.

The so-called seriocomic (*spoudaiogeloion*) was recognized as the mode most appropriate both to individual contributions to sympotic performance (cf. Agathon's conclusion at 197e7 and Alcibiades' introduction at 215a5−6) and to the symposium overall,[9] and no reader can fail to appreciate this in the *Symposium*. Xenophon too offers a picture of the sympotic Socrates—a model of moderation in the best traditions of Xenophanes—explicitly interpreting Homer in this mode:

> Whenever [Socrates] accepted an invitation to dinner, he resisted without difficulty the common temptation to exceed the limit of satiety; and he advised those who could not do likewise to avoid what was set out to make one eat when not hungry and drink when not thirsty; for he used to say that such things ruined the stomach, the brain and the soul. He said in jest that he thought that it was by offering a feast of such things that Circe turned men into pigs; Odysseus had survived this fate partly through the advice of Hermes, but also because he was self-restrained and avoided excessive indulgence in such things. This was how he spoke on such subjects, half joking (*paizôn*), half in earnest (*spoudazôn*). (Xenophon, *Memorabilia* 1.3.6−8)

There are, however, two very particular points to Plato's use of the seriocomic mode. The *Symposium* contains some of Plato's most brilliant parodic and self-parodic writing; the latter is particularly found in Socrates' hilarious account of his cross-examination by Diotima

---

[9] Cf. Xen. *Symp.* 4.28; the song of Ares and Aphrodite is described by Athenaeus as a "tale mixed with jesting, which offers advice to Odysseus on the killing of the suitors" (5.192d). For programmatic statements of this ideal, cf. Plutarch, *Sympotic Questions* 1.1 (*Moralia* 614a), 1.4 (*Moralia* 621d); Hermogenes 453−54 Rabe; Martin (1931) 2−32. *Spoudaiogeloion* was not, of course, restricted to the symposium, cf., e.g., Aristophanes, *Frogs* 391−92 (Aristophanic comedy); Plut. *Mor.* 712b−c (Menander); Horace, *Satires* 1.1.24−25 (satire).

(see p. 82). This parodic element corresponds to the half-serious, half-jesting "role playing" which could be inherent in the entertainment of a real symposium, in which the guests "performed" for the entertainment of their fellow guests. Eryximachus, Agathon, and Socrates (at least) all perform as constructed exaggerations of themselves—the theorizing doctor, the rhetorical poet, the Platonic Socrates. If these characters never let down their guard and thus role play to the end, the Platonic Alcibiades too, despite the commitment to truth which drunkenness imposes, exploits and plays up to the anecdotal tradition of "what Alcibiades was like." Unlike Ares and Aphrodite in Demodocus's song in *Odyssey* 8, Agathon's guests themselves both orchestrate and join in with the laughter they provoke. This aspect of sympotic excess, and how Plato has harnessed it, has too often eluded the moralizing critics of both antiquity and the modern day. Thus one of the guests in Athenaeus's *Sophists at Dinner* (c. 200 AD) observes that "Plato ridicules and mocks Agathon's balanced clauses and antitheses and brings on Alcibiades saying that he wants to be penetrated anally" (5.187c); what is important is not whether Alcibiades is here misrepresented or not, but rather the critic's willful misunderstanding of the nature of Plato's literary representation.

Second, in his role as a Silenus, neither man, beast, nor god (cf. below, p. 100), Socrates—funny on the outside ("throughout his whole life ironizing [*eirôneuomenos*][10] and playing with people"), supremely serious on the inside (216e4–7)—embodies the coexistence, indeed the interdependence, of the *spoudaion* and the *geloion*. Moreover, Alcibiades' description of how Socrates talks suggests that more is at stake than just an image:

> The first time a person lets himself listen to one of Socrates' arguments (*logoi*), it sounds really ridiculous. Trivial-sounding words and phrases form his arguments' outer coating, the brutal satyr's skin. He talks of pack-asses, metal-workers,

[10] The interpretation of this verb is hotly disputed; for the different views which have recently been taken, cf. Vlastos (1991) 21–44 and Nehamas (1998) 19–98.

shoemakers, tanners; he seems to go on and on using the same arguments to make the same points, with the result that ignoramuses and fools are bound to find his arguments ridiculous. But if you could see them opened up, if you can get through to what's under the surface, what you'll find inside is that his arguments are the only ones in the world which make sense. And that's not all: under the surface, his arguments abound with divinity and effigies of goodness (*aretê*). They turn out to be extremely far-reaching, or rather they cover everything which needs to be taken into consideration by someone on the path to true goodness (lit. who is going to be *kaloskagathos*). (221e1−2a6)

The charge against Socrates is a familiar one (cf. *Gorgias* 491a; *Hippias Maior* 288c−91a): irony, which invites us to interpret language in more than one way, to remove an outer layer of meaning to get at a deeper truth, is indeed one potent manifestation of the serious-playful mode. Nevertheless, we may be tempted, particularly in a work of the tone of the *Symposium*, to see this not merely as Alcibiades' enthusiastic reaction to Socratic discourse, but also as one programmatic image for the reading of Socratic dialogues as a whole, and most notably the *Symposium* itself. Alcibiades' words are an invitation to interpretation, a half-teasing come-on from Plato to his readers to find the *spoudaion* behind the amusing dress in which it has been clothed. What Alcibiades' image does not give us, of course, is a key to unlock "the meaning" of the *Symposium*: we are simply being told that reading this or any work of Plato requires effort and thought, requires us in fact to "get inside" Socrates' words (222a2). Alcibiades also holds out the promise that such effort will be more than worthwhile.

Alcibiades' image for the act of reading and interpretation was to have a long history (cf. below, pp. 129–30). In his essay "The Sileni of Alcibiades," Erasmus applied the Silenus image to both Socrates and other ancient philosophers in the Socratic mold—Antisthenes, Diogenes the Cynic, Epictetus—but, most potently of all, also to

Christ and the Christian Scriptures, on the model of Socrates and writing about Socrates:

> [S]cripture too has its own Sileni. Pause at the surface, and what you see is sometimes ridiculous; were you to pierce to the heart of the allegory, you would venerate the divine wisdom. Let us take the Old Testament. If you looked at nothing beyond the story; if you heard how Adam was made out of clay and his poor wife taken secretly out of his side while he slept, how the serpent tempted the woman . . . Yet under these wrappings, in heaven's name, how splendid is the wisdom that lies hidden! The parables in the Gospels, if you judge them by their outward shell, would be thought, surely, by everyone to be the work of an ignoramus. Crack the nutshell and of course you will find that hidden wisdom which is truly divine, something in truth very like Christ Himself.[11]

In the preface to *Gargantua*, Rabelais too borrowed the Silenus image from both Plato and Erasmus to contrast the apparently jesting titles of his works with the allegedly valuable subject matter concealed within. Like Plato, Rabelais expected his desired reader, whom he compares to a dog searching for the marrow in a bone, to work quite hard at his task.

Laughter can, of course, arise from jesting and personal mockery. The sympotic rule was that such jesting should not pass over into insulting abuse (a species of *hybris*),[12] which results not in the shared laughter which ties the whole group together but in the harsh laughter which separates the victim from his mockers. The ideal, along with the appropriate admixture of the serious, is well expressed in an anonymous poem of perhaps the later classical period:

> Hail, fellow drinkers. . . . Whenever we friends gather for such an activity, we ought to laugh and joke, behaving prop-

[11] *Collected Works of Erasmus. Adages II vii 1 to III iii 100*, translated by R. A. B. Mynors (Toronto: 1992) 267.

[12] For the jesting appropriate to symposia, cf. Plutarch, *Sympotic Questions* 1.4 (621e–22b), 2.1.

erly (lit. using *aretê*), take pleasure in being together, engage in silly talk with one another, and utter jests such as to arouse laughter. But let seriousness (*spoudê*) follow and let us listen to the speakers in their turn: this is the best form of symposium (lit. the *aretê* of the symposium). And let us obey the symposiarch: this is the conduct of good men and wins praise. (Adespota Elegiaca 27 West; trans. Gerber, adapted)

Alcibiades' jesting about Socrates' physique clearly falls well within acceptable limits, and the contrast he draws at the start of his speech, "The likeness [of Socrates to a Silenus] will be made for the sake of truth, not to raise a laugh" (215a6), is a version of the ideal of *spoudaiogeloion*. This kind of jesting unites rather than dissolves the group. When Alcibiades humorously accuses Socrates of "contempt, ridicule, and *hybris*" in passing the night in Alcibiades' arms without (apparently) any sexual arousal at all (219c), we are not to take the charges too seriously. An anecdote in Plutarch has Socrates responding to someone who asked him whether he was not upset at the *hybris* (Plutarch's word) directed against him in Aristophanes' *Clouds* with the words: "No, certainly not; I am teased (*skôptomai*) in the theater as at a large symposium" (*Moralia* 10c–d). The story is told to illustrate the philosopher's calm temperament—here is a man who collapses the distinction between public ridicule and the jesting inherent in male bonding. What the anecdote also illustrates is that the symposium is in fact private theater (cf. 194b–c) in which all the guests are both actors and appreciative audience.

More elaborate sympotic entertainments included mimes and playlets, often of an erotic and/or farcical kind.[13] The guests in Xenophon's *Symposium* are entertained by an arousing mime of the love-making of Dionysus and Ariadne. Agathon's guests, by contrast, must be content with Alcibiades' narration of his failed attempt to seduce Socrates, though this account, with its included exchange of direct speech, certainly offers plenty of scope for mimetic action; it is easy enough to imagine it as a performed "playlet" for two actors (as it might well, at some time, have been). Here, how-

[13] Cf. Davidson (2000).

ever, we are also to think of another sympotic entertainment in which Alcibiades was involved. In the period before the Athenian expedition to Sicily, Alcibiades was implicated in charges that the Eleusinian Mysteries had been profaned "in private houses" and the secrets revealed to those who had not been initiated;[14] it is a reasonable inference that what was meant was that the Mysteries had been staged as entertainment during an elite symposium.[15] Alcibiades introduces his account of the attempted seduction of Socrates in his own house (where he was charged with holding the profane ceremony) with repeated warnings that it is only for the ears of those "initiated" into Socratic rites (218b).[16] This is not only a comically down-to-earth analogy to the metaphysical "mysteries" into which Diotima begins to initiate Socrates (see pp. 92–93) but also an allusion to the serious charges which contributed to Alcibiades' loss to the Athenian cause. It is hard to see how any Athenian could fail to be reminded of such painful history, in which Phaedrus, Eryximachus, and perhaps also Eryximachus's father had all also been denounced.

Moralizing reflections and advice upon the human condition are often set within a sympotic context; much archaic poetry and various episodes in, say, Herodotus fit this pattern. The symposium was a natural setting in which to place memories of encounters with famous men: the *Epidêmiai* (Visits) of Ion of Chios (mid–fifth century BC) were first-person narratives of such meetings, and the sparse fragments suggest that a sympotic setting was common in that work. The fictional "symposium of philosophers," which gives, as Alcibiades is to do, new meaning to the proverbial wisdom that "wine reveals truth," should be seen in part as a development of this

[14] Cf. Thucydides 6.28; Lysias 6.51; Andocides, *On the Mysteries* 12; Plutarch, *Alcibiades* 19.

[15] For Alcibiades' performance as sympotic entertainment, cf. explicitly Plutarch, *Sympotic Questions* 1.4 (*Mor.* 621c); Pseudo-Heraclitus, *Homeric Problems* 76.7. Murray (1990b) 153–58 seems to wish to deny this, though it is unclear what other kind of "performance" he actually envisages.

[16] The "actions" (*prachthenta*) and "sayings" (*legomena*) of 218b5 perhaps also reflect mystic terminology (the later distinction between *drômena* and *legomena*).

tradition; the extant works of Plato and Xenophon were followed by *Symposia* of Aristotle, Speusippus, and Epicurus, to name only the best-known philosophers. Whether Plato had immediate forebears is a more difficult question.[17] The tradition of a "symposium of the Seven Sages" (the famous "wise men" of archaic Greece), best known from a work of Plutarch (which itself echoes Plato's *Symposium*), cannot certainly be traced before Plato, though Plato himself makes Socrates claim that the Sages "came together" to make dedications at Delphi (*Protagoras* 343a–b). However that may be, later sympotic literature treated Plato's work as the classic founding text of the genre, and it certainly eclipsed whatever predecessors it may have had; above all, it showed that, at a symposium, philosophy was to be served with a light touch (cf. Plutarch, *Sympotic Questions* 614d).

The symposium was, however, a central site for the transmission of a shared cultural and intellectual heritage, in other words for (male) education in the broadest social and political sense. Thus, for example, much of the elegiac poetry of Theognis of Megara (second half of sixth century BC) is set at a symposium and offers moralizing social, sexual, and political advice to a young man. It is at symposia that membership in a privileged group is both tested and acted out. Philosophical education will turn out to be at the very heart of Plato's work: the sympotic setting is thus not as frivolous as we may be tempted to believe; it is very serious indeed.

2 | erôs

By its very nature, the symposium and the poetry and literature it generated were inseparable from *erôs* and from Eros, the god who presides over and is made manifest in *erôs*. Greeks did not have our conventions of distinguishing capital and lowercase letters, which does not of course mean that they did not perceive the po-

---

[17] For the possibility of "rival accounts" of a symposium at Agathon's house, cf. below, p. 22.

tential for ambiguity, and it will become clear that this fluidity of reference will prove useful to more than one speaker in the *Symposium*. Symposiasts pursued beauty and pleasure, and women and boys were on hand to slake the desires which come with such pursuits: "savories, perfumes, incense, prostitutes, and pastries" is how the Platonic Socrates elsewhere refers to some of what made up a symposium (*Republic* 2.373a3–4). Toasts were offered to Eros as the god who could intercede with the object of one's desire, and *erôs* and its consequences are everywhere in the poetry of the brilliant symposium culture of the archaic period. The chorus of Sophocles' *Ajax* laments that the first inventor of war put an end to both symposia and *erôtes* (vv. 1199–1205).

Erôs in archaic poetry may, in the broadest terms, be thought of as an invasive force or emotion which drives one to wish to satisfy a felt need. *Erôs* demands a response; it is not an ongoing state, such as "contentment."[18] In Homer, "*erôs* for food and drink" may be easily satisfied, but the prolonged absence of food would of course lead to wasting and ultimate death. So too, in Greek poetry, *erôs* for another human being leads to physical wasting and mental distraction: *erôs* may be figured as a disease, and Aphrodite and her incarnation, the destructively beautiful Pandora, produce "longing which is hard to bear and limb-wearying cares" (Hesiod, *Works and Days* 66). Such *erôs* or *himeros* (desire) requires rapid satisfaction in sexual release, as when Paris is seized with desire instantly to make love with Helen (*Iliad* 3.441–46) or Zeus with Hera (*Iliad* 14.294–353). For the less violent "love, affection," as, for example, in the romantic modern ideal of husband-wife relationships, Homer (cf. *Iliad* 9.340–43) and later literature normally use not *erôs* and its cognates, but *philia*. In the "Ariadne and Dionysus" mime with which Xenophon's *Symposium* concludes, the sexual arousal of the couple is plain to see, but Dionysus asks his bride whether she "loves" (*philein*) him, and the guests are convinced that the couple "love (*philein*) each other" (Xenophon, *Symposium* 9.6). The mod-

[18] The account here must, necessarily, be very broad-brush. A useful introduction to many of the issues is Calame (1992); for a larger-scale study of the semantics of *erôs*, cf. Ludwig (2002).

ern English "I love you" is normally *philô se*, though the statement itself may be prompted not by *philia* but by *erôs*. When in book 1 of Herodotus, King Candaules "felt *erôs* for his own wife," this extraordinary infatuation leads to his death and loss of the throne (Hdt. 1.8). *Erôs* is very often a response to visual beauty—another idea which the *Symposium* will turn to its own ends—but in turn it affects the very way we see: Sappho's declaration that "whatever one loves is most beautiful (*kalon*)" (fr. 16.3–4) was to have a very long afterlife in proverbial wisdom.

As *erôs* is an invasive force from outside, its presence can be shaming and disorienting, in that it takes away one's better judgment and one's sense of independence; *erôs* forces us to confront our lack and need, ideas which are to be fundamental to the *Symposium*. *Erôs*, moreover, regularly forces people to do things which they, in more considered moments, know to be wrong or socially disapproved; it is traditionally an irrational power which works against the better counsels of reason. The catastrophic outcome of the Athenian expedition to Sicily is foreshadowed in the fact that the citizens felt a powerful *erôs* for the venture (Thucydides 6.24.3). In Euripides' *Medea*, the self-serving Jason argues that Medea can take no credit for saving the Argonautic expedition because she was acting under the compulsion of *erôs*, which takes the place of personal responsibility (*Medea* 526–31), and in the *Trojan Women* Helen uses a similar argument to exculpate herself for having left Sparta with Paris (vv. 945–50). Before Plato, Attic tragedy had indeed explored the destructiveness of *erôs* with particular power. "Terrible desire" for a beautiful girl (v. 476) led Heracles to sack her city and set in motion the chain of events of Sophocles' *Trachiniae*; both Heracles' wife herself and the chorus must acknowledge that everyone, including the gods, is defenseless before the power of *erôs* (vv. 441–44, 497–502; cf. *Antigone* 781–800). In Euripides' *Hippolytus*, Phaedra explains her doomed attempts to overcome by self-control (*sôphrosynê*, v. 399) the "terrible *erôs*" (v. 28), whose ravaging, "body-untying" (v. 199) effects are all too clear as she is first carried in. It is Phaedra's knowledge of her own predicament (cf. vv. 504–6) and her ability to reason about it which construct her tragedy.

Erôs, of course, is also responsible for the continuation of the human race (cf. Euripides, *Hippolytus* 449–50) and can bring great pleasure, but one must pray to avoid its full destructive force (cf. *Hippolytus* 528–29). As such, it deserves to be treated with full cult honors, and the chorus of the *Hippolytus* (vv. 535–42) anticipates the Platonic Aristophanes' surprise at the absence of major cults of Eros (*Symposium* 189c5–9). This doubleness in the power of *erôs* brings it close to Dionysus, whose principal manifestation among men—wine—is similarly double-edged and whose destructive potential was celebrated in many myths. "It is a bad thing to drink a lot of wine, but if one drinks it with understanding, it is not bad but good" (Theognis 509–10).[19] The problem, of course, as the Greeks knew only too well, was how difficult such understanding was: as wine is drunk, it takes over the drinker's judgment, so that the "decision" to drink more (or less), just like sexual arousal, is no real "decision" at all. The "middle way" in both drinking (cf., e.g., Theognis 837–40) and desire (cf., e.g., Euripides, *Hippolytus* 525–32) is not an easy path to tread. Dionysus's wine, like *erôs*, enters from the outside and works its changes upon both mind and body; that, moreover, alcohol stimulates sexual desire was as familiar to the ancients as it is to us, and the two are constantly found together in poetry and narrative. In the second century AD the novelist Achilles Tatius put it thus:

> Once Eros and Dionysus, two forceful gods, have gripped the soul, they drive it to ecstatic shamelessness, the one burning it with his usual flame, the other providing the fuel in the form of wine (for wine is the food of desire). (Achilles Tatius 2.3.3; trans. T. Whitmarsh)

The *Symposium* emphasizes Socrates' imperviousness to the effects of wine (220a4–5), as well as his indifference to its pleasures (176c3–5). After drinking all night, he is found conducting a very typical "So-

[19] For the explicit comparison of drunkenness to desire, cf. Plutarch, *Moralia* 622d–e.

cratic" dialectic about knowledge and craft (223d; cf. below, p. 79) and then has a perfectly normal day (223d10). It is, moreover, not just alcohol which appears to have no effect upon him: having the beautiful Alcibiades in his bed has no obvious effect upon either his mind or his body. Under the influence of desire and/or Dionysus, Socrates remains as changeless and unaffected as we will learn the Form of Beauty itself to be (211a–b). Viewed from another perspective, however, Diotima's speech will suggest that *erôs*, properly understood, governs Socrates' whole life and his pursuit of philosophical understanding.

All of the speeches of the *Symposium* are predominantly concerned with the *erôs* felt by an adult man, the *erastês* (lover), for a younger man, the *erômenos* (he who is loved, the beloved); the *erômenos* in such relationships was usually adolescent or somewhat older. The Greek term for these social practices is "boy-love" (*paiderastia*), but it is important that, in Greek, this term does not carry the strongly negative associations of modern "pederasty"; in this book, "pederasty," "pederastic," and related words refer to Greek practice and are (as far as I can make them) value-free. These practices have, of course, always been at the center of debates about the value and values of Greek society (cf. below, pp. 114–25). Greek sexuality, in all its complexity, has been much studied in recent years, and the bibliography contains reading suggestions for those wishing to pursue histories and explanations of Greek sexual practices.

The *Symposium* is one of a series of fourth-century prose works devoted to the pleasures and pains and nature of *erôs*; the *Symposium* is in fact referred to as Plato's *erôtikoi logoi* (erotic speeches) as early as Aristotle (*Politics* 2.1262b11). Other surviving examples of the genre include parts of Plato's *Phaedrus*, a treatise on *erôs* ascribed to Demosthenes, and the "love story" of Panthea which opens the fifth book of Xenophon's *Cyropaideia*. The theme, which was to become a dominant one in the New Comedy of Menander, occurs already in fourth-century comedy in forms which perhaps suggest the influence of the prose discussions of Plato and others. The comic poet Alexis explicitly associates the idea that not Eros but lovers fly with "wise men" (*sophistai*; fr. 20 Kassel-Austin), and in another passage from a comedy, perhaps significantly entitled "Phaedrus," a lover reflects on the nature of his experience in ways which bring us close to the *Symposium*:

> As I was coming from the Peiraeus my troubles and lack of resource led me to philosophical reflection. To put it very briefly, I think that all the painters who make images of Eros are unfamiliar with this *daimôn*. He is neither female nor male, neither god nor man, neither brainless nor again wise, but he is a mixture of all different things and carries many forms with him in one shape. He has the daring of a man, the cowardice of a woman, the foolishness of madness, the arguments (*logos*) of a wise man, the vehemence of a beast, is unremittingly hard-working, and being a god (*daimôn*) loves to be honoured. (Alexis fr. 247 Kassel-Austin)

3 | Telling the Story

The opening conversation establishes a complex history for the account of Agathon's symposium:

APOLLODORUS: I think I'm quite an expert (lit. not unpracticed) in what you're asking about. I mean, just the other day I was on my way up to town from my home in Phalerum and an acquaintance of mine spotted me from behind and called out to me—he was some way off. He used his raised voice as an opportunity to have a bit of fun: "Hey you!" he shouted. "You Phalerian there! Apollodorus! Wait for me, won't you?"

I stopped and waited for him to catch up. "You know, Apollodorus," he said, "I was looking for you only the other day. I wanted to ask you what happened at that party which Agathon, Socrates, Alcibiades, and all the other guests were at, and to find out how their speeches on love went. I've already had a report from someone else (who'd been told about it by Phoenix the son of Philip), but his account wasn't very clear. He did mention, though, that you knew about it as well. So please will you tell me? I mean, Socrates is your friend, so it's perfectly appropriate for you to report what he says. But tell me first," he added, "whether or not you were actually there when they met."

"It certainly looks as though you've heard a garbled version of the story," I said, "if you're under the impression that the party you're asking about took place a short while ago, and so that I could have been there."

"Yes, I did think that," he said.

"But how could I have been, Glaucon?" I asked. "Agathon hasn't lived here in Athens for many years, you know, and it's less than three years since I've been among Socrates' companions and have been making it my business to know, day by day, what he says and does. It's only been that long since I stopped my pointless running around. I used to think I was getting somewhere, when I was worse off than anyone—well, just as badly off as you are now, since you'd rather do anything than do philosophy."

"Don't tease," he said. "Just tell me, please, when it was that they *did* all meet."

"When you and I were still boys," I replied. "Agathon had won with his first tragedy, and they met on the day after he and the cast had performed the victory rites."

"It really was a long time ago, then," he said. "But who told you the story? Was it Socrates himself?"

"Oh, good heavens, no!" I exclaimed. "It was the same person who told Phoenix about it. He's called Aristodemus—from the deme of Cydathenaeum, a little fellow, never wears shoes. He'd been there at the party, since he was one of the greatest lovers Socrates had at the time, I think. All the same, I did also ask Socrates about some of what Aristodemus told me, and the two accounts coincided." (172a1–73b6)

The information which Apollodorus provides may be displayed in the same genealogical manner in which relationships of descent between manuscripts are often set out (all versions of Agathon's symposium, except, of course, Apollodorus's, are "lost"). See figure 1.

The alleged existence of a rival account of Agathon's party, though one traceable ultimately to the same source, is both the kind of realistic detail which we recognize as one of the hallmarks of fiction—news of the closed world of a symposium may indeed often have reached the outside only through gossip and rumor: "I hate a drinking companion (*sympotas*) with a memory," says a Greek proverb[20]—and a warning which should put us on our guard. Apollodorus's paraded concern with historical accuracy, and the procedures for procuring it, advertise the fictionality of the account in a pleasing paradox. Historical accuracy may not, in any event, be the right criterion to judge the narrative we are about to read; the vagueness of the dramatic date of the conversation between Apollodorus and his friend (above p. 4) is one of many signs of this. The question of whether or not Plato does in fact have his eyes on one or more earlier "Socratic symposia" by authors whose names are now lost to us must not obscure the literary purpose of his chosen narrative mode. Plato's various experiments with narrative frames[21] show his persistent concern to advertise and problematize the fictional status of his dialogues. Thus, the *Parmenides* reaches us through a series of four "sources," beginning with an eyewitness (Zeno himself); in the *Theaetetus*, Eukleides claims to have received the account directly from Socrates and, through repeated questionings of the philosopher, has "practically the whole story written out" (143a5); the *Phaedo* is related by Phaedo, an eyewitness of events (*autos* [yourself] is the first word of the dialogue; contrast

[20] Plutarch, *Sympotic Questions* 686b–d, earnestly notes with pleasure that philosophers' symposia are an exception to the usual rule, because one can remember (and read) what was said the night before. The same proverbial idea is also given prominence at the start of Lucian's *Symposium* (chap. 3), as that work also begins with an imitation of the elaborate "sourcing" of Apollodorus's account of Agathon's party.

[21] Cf., e.g., Clay (1992); Johnson (1998).

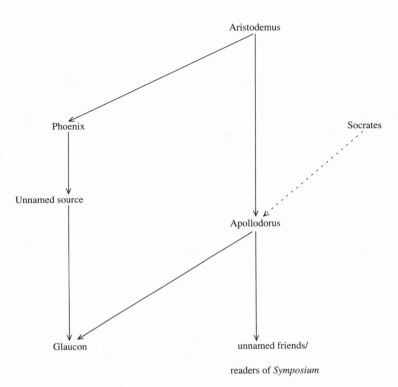

FIGURE I

Symposium 172b8), to his host in Phlius who seeks a clear (*saphês*) and detailed (*akribês*) account of what happened, just as Glaucon does from Apollodorus.

The body of the *Symposium*, like that of the *Parmenides*, is consistently in indirect speech or, rather, the *narrative* is indirect, that is, "and then [Aristodemus said that] Socrates said," whereas the speeches themselves are reported in direct speech; this is a mode of presentation which never lets us forget that we are not being offered unmediated access to a "true account" of "what happened" in Agathon's house. Moreover, Aristodemus and Apollodorus have both imperfect memories and a practice of selectivity over which we have

no control (178a1—5, 180c2, 223c7); from what we have learned of
Apollodorus we would not necessarily rely on his judgment as to
what was "worthy of record" (178a2), and Aristodemus falls asleep
just when things are getting interesting (223b8—9). Plato's explicit
interest in problems of narrative mode is clear from a famous discussion in the third book of the *Republic* (392c6 ff.) in which Socrates
divides narrative into "simple *diêgêsis*" (where the poet tells everything in the third person), "mimetic *diêgêsis*" (where, as in drama,
everything happens through the words of "characters"), and "mixed
diêgêsis" (which, like epic poetry, partakes of both forms); so too, in
the *Theaetetus*, Eukleides explains how he has turned what he has
learned into "direct speech" (or, perhaps, into a drama) by omitting
all the "he told me that he replied's" and so forth (*Theaetetus* 143b5—
c6). It is possible, in fact, that something of the sort also occurs in
the *Symposium*. Socrates' report of his conversation with Diotima
takes place within the overarching frame of indirect and direct
speech described above, but is itself almost (cf. 201e2—7) entirely in
direct speech; Socrates' initial stress, however, upon the fidelity of
his reproduction of the discussion (201d5—e2; cf. below, p. 82)
perhaps includes the dramatic form of what is to follow, in the manner of the introduction to the *Theaetetus*. Nevertheless, despite these
clear analogies elsewhere in the Platonic corpus, we may still feel
that the nested narrative of the *Symposium* requires more explanation than simply Platonic interest in narrative experimentation.

The narrator, Apollodorus, "spends his time with Socrates and
makes it his business to know all that he says or does every day"
(172e5—7; cf. Xenophon, *Memorabilia* 3.11.17). In other words, for
him Socrates is not merely a respected guide, but is a kind of guru
on whose every word he hangs. Moreover, Apollodorus tells us that
before his conversion to Socrates and philosophy he "ran around
in any old direction," thinking that anything was more important
than philosophy.[22] Stories of conversion to philosophy are common

---

[22] Later stories of the "conversion" of Plato himself to philosophy most commonly make him a poet in his youth; cf. Riginos (1976) 43—48.

from the later Hellenistic world, with its institutionalization of competing philosophical schools, and such stories often represent conversion as a change from movement and hurry to stability and fixedness (of which the Socrates of the *Symposium* is, of course, a prime model). Polemon, head of Plato's Academy in the late fourth century, provides an excellent example:

> Polemon's father, Philostratus, was one of the leading men of Athens and used to race chariots. It is said that when Polemon was a young man he was a loose-liver (*akolastos*) and once when drunk went on a revel through the Kerameikos in the middle of the day. He was scandalously indicted by his wife for abusive treatment, for he was fond of boys and young men. He used to carry coins around with him so that he would be able to have instant sex with anyone he met. When however he had been captivated by Xenocrates [the head of the Academy] and spent time with him, he so changed his life that he never again altered his countenance or his bearing or the tone of his voice, but kept them the same even when he was in a very bad mood.[23]

Here is a vision of what Alcibiades, the very embodiment of horse racing, drunken escapades, and erotic adventures, could have become had he stayed still beside Socrates; instead he bursts in and out of the lives of others, and neither he nor his emotions ever have time to rest quietly (216b2–c3).

Neither Aristodemus nor Apollodorus were, as far as we know, a great gain for the progress of philosophy, though both knew how to go through the motions. Apollodorus's mixture of contempt and

---

[23] Philodemus on the authority of Antigonus of Carystus; cf. K. Gaiser, *Philodems Academica* (Stuttgart: 1988) 230–33. In another version of the same material (Diogenes Laertius 4.16), Polemon, "drunk and wearing a garland," bursts into a lecture of Xenocrates on *sôphrosynê* (in imitation of the Platonic Alcibiades?). It is worth noting that, according to Antigonus, Polemon "imitated Xenocrates in everything" (Gaiser op. cit. 240; cf. Diogenes Laertius 4.19)—another narrative element of importance for Aristodemus and Apollodorus.

pity for what he once was and for "nonphilosophers," particularly those involved in the real world of power and money (173c6), may however remind us of Lucretius's Epicurean self-satisfaction:

> Nothing is more sweet than to dwell in the calm regions, firmly embattled on the heights by the teaching of the wise, whence you can look down on others, and see them wandering hither and thither, going astray as they seek the way of life, in strife matching their wits or rival claims of birth, struggling night and day by surpassing effort to rise up to the height of power and gain possession of the world. Ah! Miserable minds of men, blind hearts! (Lucretius, *De rerum natura* 2.7–14; trans. Bailey, adapted)

or of Seneca's regret at wasted opportunities:

> So long as we wander aimlessly, having no guide, and following only the noise and discordant cries of those who call us in different directions, life will be consumed in making mistakes—life that is brief even if we should strive day and night for sound wisdom. Let us, therefore, decide both upon the goal and upon the way, and not fail to find some experienced guide who has explored the region towards which we are advancing. . . . (Seneca, *De vita beata* 1.2; trans. Basore)

Apollodorus has certainly found his guide, though whether he understands what that guide has to say is (at least) a moot point. Moreover, as we shall see, the practice of Socratic philosophy is inimical to the idea of the master whose teaching imparts wisdom: this is the message of what Socrates jokingly tells Agathon when he first arrives (175d), and it is what Alcibiades too failed to understand. Alcibiades thought that, by offering himself to Socrates, he could "hear everything that Socrates knew" (217a5), but the getting of wisdom is not a matter of facile exchange, as Socrates points out to him (218e–19a; cf. below, p. 107).

Plato's various experiments with narrative form are all, at different levels, concerned with patterns of tradition and authority, and (with hindsight) may be seen to reflect upon the formation of philosophical "schools"; such experiments are also, of course, ways of dealing with Plato's own paradoxical position as a recorder, after Socrates' death, of Socrates' unwritten words. Apollodorus, who is described at the opening of the *Phaedo* as particularly affected by the coming death of Socrates (59a9–b4; cf. Xenophon, *Apology* 28), is in the *Symposium* a comically ironized picture of "the author" (Plato) himself, just as the short,[24] barefooted Aristodemus is a slightly absurd imitation of Socrates. Although "Socrates" may sometimes function as a kind of shorthand for philosophy to be a "lover of Socrates" (173b3) is not, as the case of Alcibiades will show most painfully, to be a "lover of wisdom," that is, a philosopher. So too, the chain of information from Aristodemus to Apollodorus to his unnamed acquaintances is an oblique and ironical representation of the constructed chain from Socrates to Plato to Plato's readers (ancient and modern), who are interested in Socrates but need not be serious philosophers. The implied question which we must imagine to have preceded the opening of the work, "What happened at that symposium at Agathon's house?" evokes the curiosity and expectation which make us start reading the text.

Plato, moreover, likes to signal his presence in the text behind the characters. Thus, for example, at the start of the dialogue named after him, Phaedo welcomes the opportunity to tell the story of Socrates' last hours: "Remembering Socrates is for me the greatest of pleasures, both when I am speaking and when I am listening to another" (*Phaedo* 58d5–6; cf. *Symp.* 215d3–4). In the *Symposium*, the sources for our narrative, our "remembering Socrates," are drawn with particular sharpness. Just as Aristodemus copies Socrates, as though appearance alone could make a philosopher, so Apollodorus, whose opening anecdote might even be construed as a (poor) imitation of the opening of the Platonic *Republic*,[25] has nothing of his own to contribute to philosophy, except the (allegedly) verbatim repetition of the *logoi* of others. Both of these imitations fall well

[24] Xenophon, *Memorabilia* 1.4.2 makes "Shorty" a nickname for Aristodemus.

[25] Cf., e.g., Rosen (1987) 11–13; Rowe (1998) 127. The relative chronology implied by this speculation is, of course, disputed.

short of "doing philosophy," as in particular Diotima's speech (itself an allegedly verbatim repetition by Socrates in teasing, carnivalesque mood) will demonstrate. Apollodorus, like all those who wrote positively about Socrates after his death, is open to the charge of being entirely uncritical (in both senses) in his attitude toward Socrates (173d4−10). Is Plato liable to this charge? Perhaps, but Plato calls attention to his own crucial difference both from Apollodorus (Plato has his own philosophical contributions to make) and from Socrates (Plato writes). Plato's biographical concern with Socrates' every move may seem no less than Apollodorus's, but the Platonic Socrates, unlike the Apollodoran, is an idea, a figure of fiction and myth "with which to think," not an attempt at historically accurate biography (cf. below, pp. 110−11).[26]

Philosophical schools need ways of keeping in touch with the revered figures of the past, but Socrates left nothing in writing; he is, therefore, in a special sense the creation of those who write about him. When we are told that he confirmed some of the details of Aristodemus's account (173b5−6), we may be tempted not just to see him (and Plato) having a joke at Apollodorus's passion for accuracy (without understanding), but also to see an acknowledgment by Plato, who could no longer check the reliability of his "sources" with Socrates, of the fictionality of his *Symposium*.[27] It is for Plato not a question of one account being more historically accurate than another, but of the very nature of the fictional construct which is "Socrates" and his life. Moreover, Apollodorus's own *epideixis* is "not

[26] Cf. Nussbaum (1986) 168: "Socrates' pupils, inspired by personal love, tend not to follow his advice. Instead of ascending to an equal regard for all instances of value, they, like Alcibiades, remain lovers of the particulars of personal history." For a helpful discussion of Platonic and other representations of Socrates, cf. Blondell (2002) 85−112.

[27] Rowe (1998) 4−5 sees the point of Apollodorus's claim to have checked details with Socrates in the idea that "[the historical] Socrates would not have demurred from what he is supposed to have believed on the authority of 'Diotima.' . . . the ideas in question are to be taken seriously." For another important approach to this passage, see Halperin (1992) 111.

unrehearsed" (*ameletêtos*, the opening line of the work) — it is in fact a repetition, perhaps indeed a verbatim repetition, of what was in any case originally a repetition of Aristodemus's report; we may be reminded of how Phaedrus hoped to give an oral performance of Lysias's speech as the result of much secret practice (*meletê*) from a written script (*Phaedrus* 228a–b).[28] As Socrates famously points out in the *Phaedrus*, a written text can never answer questions, it can only repeat itself over and over again. Thus, the framing fiction of the *Symposium* highlights its problematic status as a written, unchanging account of a quintessentially oral occasion, the elite symposium. It is a provocation to reflection, not — so we are to understand — a "master text" to be learned by heart and endlessly repeated.

4 | Displaying Wisdom

Aristodemus said that he happened to meet Socrates under unusual circumstances — bathed and wearing shoes! He asked him where he was going, all smartened up like that.

"I'm going to dinner at Agathon's," Socrates replied. "You see, I didn't like the look of the crowd yesterday at the victory celebration, so I kept away from him there; but I promised to be there today. That's why I've tricked myself out: he's good-looking (*kalos*), and I must look good when I visit him. What about you?" he asked. "How do you feel about coming to a dinner uninvited? Would you be prepared to do that?"

"Whatever you say," Aristodemus replied.

"Come with me, then," Socrates said, "and we'll distort and alter the proverb, to show that in fact 'Good men go of their own accord to good men's feasts.' I mean, Homer's not far off actually brutalizing the proverb, let alone distorting

---

[28] Cf. *Parmenides* 126c2–7, where we are told that the immediate source of the account we are to hear, Antiphon, learned it by heart with considerable effort when he was a young man.

it: in his poem Agamemnon is an exceptionally good man—good at warfare—and Menelaus is a 'feeble fighter' [*Iliad* 17.588], yet when Agamemnon is performing a ritual sacrifice and hosting a celebration, Homer has Menelaus coming uninvited to the feast [*Iliad* 2.408]—a worse man to a better man's feast."

In response to this Aristodemus said, "Actually, I too may fit the Homeric situation rather than the one you're imagining, Socrates, since I'm of no consequence and I'm going uninvited to a clever (*sophos*) man's feast. So you'd better think up an excuse for bringing me, because I won't admit to coming uninvited; I'll tell them you invited me!"

"'The two of us travelling together up the road' [*Iliad* 10.224] will plan our lines," Socrates replied. "Let's go." (174a3–d3)

So begins Apollodorus's account of Agathon's party. Most unusually, Socrates is all dressed up, no longer the barefoot, scruffy nuisance of the comic stage,[29] nor the ascetic figure already familiar to Plato's readers from earlier dialogues,[30] but rather a character cleaned up and made to look (from one angle) like a member of polite society, if still a bit comic in his best shoes. This is, so we are to understand, Socrates' paradoxical, but appropriately carnivalesque, response to the Dionysiac moment represented by the symposium. In wearing his "party clothes," Socrates physically embodies the literary form of this most festive dialogue, in which philosophy puts on its party face. Alcibiades will repeatedly warn us that we have to look for the beauty which lies concealed within Socrates' ugly outer appearance and his ridiculously common vocabulary (lit. the language in which his *logoi* are clothed; 221e1–4; see p. 11); when the

[29] Cf. Aristophanes, *Clouds* 103, 363 (shoelessness); *Clouds* 442, 836–87, *Birds* 1554 (dirt).

[30] For the relative chronology of the *Symposium*, cf. above, p. 3. The *Symposium* constantly exploits our familiarity with other Socratic writings, both that of Plato and of others; it is this simple fact, not the details of chronology, which it is important to grasp.

man himself is spruced up (lit. having made himself *kalos*), we must really be on our guard.

If we can detect some good-natured teasing in Aristodemus's opening question, we might also come to recognize both the shadow of a genuinely Socratic problem ("What is the nature of beauty?"; cf. Xenophon, *Symposium* 5.1–10), which will prove central to Diotima's disquisition (cf. esp. 210e–12a),[31] and a role confusion which is to be important later in the dialogue. *Kalos* (beautiful) is the standard term for an *erômenos*, a young man who is the object of an older male's affections, and Alcibiades will tell us how he, paradoxically, had to play the "lover" (*erastês*) to Socrates' *erômenos* in his efforts to acquire Socrates' wisdom. This, then, is not the last time in the *Symposium* in which Socrates will play the dandy. Socrates has, moreover, already entered into the spirit of the elite symposium— he shuns the crowd (174a7), but is prepared to attend a select gathering, and his conversation is laced with puns,[32] jokingly twisted proverbs, and Homeric quotations and interpretations. The deliberately tendentious Homeric interpretation, which may be intended as a joking example of the contemporary critical practices of the elite symposium,[33] exposes the reality that truth is the object neither of

---

[31] Lowenstam (1985) argues that the question of whether it is the "beautiful" or the "nonbeautiful" who approach the beautiful and good (*agathon*) is what prompts Socrates' immediately following bout of silent introspection, during which he works out what he subsequently shares with the other guests as Diotima's speech; cf. also Kahn (1996) 340. The idea has its attractions, but the absence of any reference to *erôs* at this early stage makes it ultimately unconvincing. A key thing about Socrates is that no one ever knows what he is thinking about.

[32] It is at least worth remarking that the notice of Agathon's departure from Athens at Aristophanes, *Frogs* 83–85 shares with Plato the pun upon *agathos* and a reference to a "feast of the blessed"; how much traditional material about this poet does Plato draw upon?

[33] Athenaeus's guests discuss this same passage of Homer and Plato's discussion of it (5.177c–79e); it is instructive about ancient criticism that, whereas Athenaeus defends Menelaus on the perfectly proper ground that the insult is spoken by Apollo to Hector, not in the voice of the poet, he (or his anti-Platonic sources) take no account of the fact that in Plato the speaker is the jesting Socrates. For "literary criticism" and the symposium, cf. Slater (1982).

epic poetry nor of its interpretation, and the cultural claims of poetry are indeed to be the object of sustained irony in the *Symposium*.

Before Agathon's door has been reached, however, the old Socrates has reasserted himself; a change of clothes does not change the man. Socrates seems preoccupied and tells Aristodemus to go ahead, with the result that the latter comes alone into the company of Agathon and his guests, where he is greeted with exemplary courtesy (174d7–75a). Aristodemus recognizes this pattern—Socrates sometimes just withdraws and stands still (175b1–2)—and urges Agathon to leave him alone, as he will eventually turn up, which indeed (without a word of explanation) he does. Later, Alcibiades is to tell of another occasion when Socrates stood, self-absorbed, for more than twenty-four hours while an audience of his fellow soldiers gathered to watch him (220c3–d5). Alcibiades interprets this behavior as a sign that Socrates was searching for the answer to a problem which took him a very long time; so too, he reports that the soldiers spread the word that Socrates was "thinking something over." Socrates himself, however, offers no account of his behavior, and though we might be tempted to interpret it as "the philosopher . . . thinking things through by himself" (Rowe on 174d5) or the "concentrated intellectual scrutiny of a problem" (Dover on 220c4), Socrates' lack of explanation itself is important. At a banal level, the timing of the first "withdrawal" makes the point that Agathon's dinner party is not, for Socrates, an all-consuming object of interest (contrast the passion with which subsequent reports of it are pursued by Apollodorus, Glaucon, and others); indeed it brings no real change in his routine at all, as the end of the dialogue makes clear. It is easy to see how such behavior could be marked down as another example of Socrates' nonconformist refusal to behave like ordinary people (cf. the soldiers at 220b7–8), but it is not, as the first instance at least makes clear, directed at an audience; there are no grounds for thinking that Socrates wants to put Agathon and his guests in their place or to make a public demonstration of "what a philosopher looks like." When the soldiers gather to watch Socrates, he (apparently) takes no notice, and they are of no significance to the outcome.

Such periods of silent self-absorption are the closest Socrates comes to public display, or *epideixis*,[34] or rather they constitute one, peculiarly Socratic and self-directed, form of what may seem to an observer to be a "performance." Agathon's art, by contrast, is precisely built upon success with a (mass) audience. When Agathon jokingly asks Socrates to sit beside him, so that, through contact, he can benefit from whatever "piece of wisdom" Socrates has acquired while standing in the neighbors' porch (175d1−2), Socrates counters with an exaggerated eulogy of Agathon's wisdom which "shone brilliantly the other day before more than 30,000 Greek witnesses" (175e5−6). Their very different "wisdoms" are acknowledged by Alcibiades, who will crown them both, as he plays the role of Dionysus predicted by Agathon at 175e9. Agathon's "displays" (*epideixeis*; cf. 194b3) are both very public and, unlike Socrates' inner-directed reflections, directed precisely to the public. His performance at his own symposium, which he himself likens to a theater (194a6), will be no less aimed at a particular audience. Nor, of course, is drama the only kind of *epideixis* which may be contrasted in this way with Socrates' behavior.

Doctors too were in the habit of giving public "displays" of their talents, in part to attract clients, and Eryximachus's "performance" should be seen in that light (cf. below, p. 54). Great intellectuals and sophists, such as Prodicus (cf. the famous "Choice of Heracles," 177b2−4), Gorgias (cf. Plato, *Hippias Maior* 282b−c), and, from an earlier generation, Protagoras, gave public displays of their learning, whether through set speeches, such as Protagoras's great *epideixis* at Plato, *Protagoras* 320c8−28d2, or by taking questions from the audience, or by a mixture of the two modes (cf. Plato, *Gorgias* 447c5−8). Paradoxical argument, such as, for example, that of the nonlover in the *Phaedrus* who argues that a young man should show sexual gratitude to a man who does not love him rather than to one who does, is another way in which the ingenuity of the speaker may be advertised. Among the things which unite these forms are their

[34] On *epideixis* as characteristic of the late fifth−early fourth century, cf., e.g., Thomas (2000) 250−69; Thomas (2003), with further bibliography.

potential to reach a wide audience and their hierarchical structure: power, often in the form of knowledge, is here very clearly in the hands of the performer. It may often seem to modern readers that the Socrates of many Platonic dialogues exercises a similar performative power and plays to the audience no less than do the sophists, as he protests his ignorance and reduces his interlocutors to helpless confusion. There is, however, a fundamental difference between, on the one hand, both his periods of "abstraction" and his practice of dialectic and, on the other, "displays" of brilliance and superficial knowledge; in the *Symposium*, the contrast is clear in Socrates' questioning of Agathon which immediately follows the latter's performance and in Diotima's reported questioning of the young Socrates.

The form of *epideixis* which lies at the heart of the *Symposium* is, of course, that of encomium or praise (*epainos*), a form fully developed in poetry before prose (cf. 177a–d), a fact perhaps reflected in the poet Agathon's triumphant *jeu d'esprit*.[35] The symposium was certainly a traditional site for encomia, both poetic and not, of beautiful young men, and Phaedrus's shift from praise of individual *erômenoi* to that of *erôs* itself foreshadows the move of Diotima/ Socrates from the particular to the universal (cf. below, p. 93). Moreover, Diotima's description of the "far from beautiful" Eros (203c6–7) and Alcibiades' praise (*epainos*, 215a4) of the old and ugly Socrates are to be seen as striking adaptations of a traditional form. Plato himself elsewhere refers to encomiastic works (in both poetry and prose) praising the family and wealth of an *erômenos* (*Lysis* 204d– 5d) or a powerful aristocrat (*Theaetetus* 174e–5b), and such compositions were no doubt very common.

Epideictic encomium was, moreover, an important manifestation of the increased professionalization and education in rhetorical techniques which characterized classical Athens. What is probably the earliest surviving treatise on rhetorical techniques, the so-called

---

[35] On the history of the encomium and its relation to such forms as the hymn, cf. Nightingale (1995) 93–106; Hunter (2003) 8–24 with further bibliography.

Rhetoric to Alexander (mid–fourth century?), sets out a clear formula for writing encomia:

> After the introduction one should make a distinction be-
> tween the goods external to virtue and those actually inher-
> ent in virtue, putting it thus: goods external to virtue fall
> under high birth, strength, beauty and wealth; virtue is di-
> vided into wisdom, justice, courage and creditable habits.
> Those belonging to virtue are justly eulogised, but those ex-
> ternal to it are kept in the background since it is appropriate
> for the strong and handsome and well-born and rich to re-
> ceive not praise but congratulation. Having then made this
> distinction, we shall place first after the introduction the ge-
> nealogy of the person we are speaking of, as that is the fun-
> damental ground of reputation or discredit for human be-
> ings, and also for animals; so in eulogising a human being
> or a domestic animal we shall state their pedigree, although
> when praising an emotion or action or speech or possession
> we shall base our approval directly on the creditable quali-
> ties that actually belong to it. (*Rhetoric to Alexander* 1440b16–
> 28; trans. H. Rackham)

After describing the method of praising the family of the subject of the speech, the author then advises a roughly chronological pro-gression through the subject's life which highlights and magnifies the accomplishments of each stage of development. The accom-plishments of adult life are to be divided according to the parts of virtue: justice, wisdom, courage, and so on (1441b3–13). To a greater or lesser extent, all the speeches in the *Symposium* show elements of these formal patterns, though none simply reproduces a scholastic formula. Thus, for example, Alcibiades' idiosyncratic encomium of Socrates focuses upon the "cardinal virtues" of wisdom, modera-tion (*sôphrosynê*), and bravery.

The author of the *Rhetoric* envisages encomia not just of humans but also of "other living creatures" (prize-winning horses? 1440b25–27), and Phaedrus (as quoted by Eryximachus) complains that he has come across a written encomium of salt and that there are many other such things available (177b5–6). The reason for composing such "half-joking, half-serious" works is clear: what is important in such works is the verbal and intellectual facility of the composer, not the substance or importance of the thing praised; such compositions are, in fact, a means of praising the speaker, not the subject. For Plato this is all part of the mendacity of a contemporary rhetorical practice which is consistently portrayed throughout his works as having no interest in truth or moral value. If this mendacity is treated with appropriate lightheartedness in the festive *Symposium*, the issue remains deadly serious; in the attack upon the *spoudaiogeloion*, it is the *spoudaiogeloion* itself which is the principal weapon.

Eryximachus proposes that each guest should offer "the most beautiful (*kalliston*) speech in praise of Eros which he can manage" (177d2–3), thus (unwittingly) placing the emphasis, as with encomia of salt, upon the skill of the speaker, not upon the value of what is said. Socrates picks this up with his insistent reference to the beauty of Agathon's speech (198b2, 4), but immediately makes the point, again with typical irony, that he now realizes that encomium has nothing to do with truth, but with ascribing every possible beauty and virtue to the thing being praised, and as such it is a form with which he can have nothing to do (198c6–99a6).[36] A commitment to truth introduces Socrates' contribution to the symposium (199a7), and at its conclusion he jokingly suggests that Phaedrus may not wish to call his performance an encomium to Love, presumably because its focus has been on truth, not upon laudation without regard to truth (212c1–3). The rejection of encomium, as having nothing to do with truth, is of a piece with the Platonic Socrates' rejection of "rhetoric" elsewhere, most notably in the *Gorgias*, as aiming not at true understanding, but merely at the persuasion and gratification of an otherwise ignorant audience; in the real world,

---

[36] Cf. Socrates' ironic formula for a funeral speech at *Menexenus* 235a1–2. The "beautiful words" with which, according to Socrates, such speeches are tricked out contrast with the allegedly random vocabulary and arrangement of Socrates' contribution to the *Symposium* (199b4–5).

political and forensic oratory may have far more damaging consequences than undeserved praise, but at the heart of both lies the same corrosive unconcern with truth and value. Alongside the light-hearted banter of the *Symposium*, we may place the rather more serious tone of the opening of the *Apology* in which Socrates contrasts the persuasive but entirely untruthful speeches of his prosecutors with the simple truth, delivered in ordinary words and ordinary Socratic mode, which they shall hear from him (*Apology* 17a–c; cf. *Symposium* 199b2–5).

·2·

Erôs before Socrates

1 | Phaedrus

Phaedrus, who begins the series of encomia, came from a wealthy Athenian family and is characterized in Plato by an interest in clever argument: in the *Protagoras* we find him, together with his friend Eryximachus, putting questions on natural science to the sophist Hippias (*Protagoras* 315c5−6), and in the dialogue named after him he has been captivated by an epideictic speech of Lysias, in which a man seeks to persuade an *erômenos* that he should give his sexual favors to someone who does not love him rather than to someone who does. So too in the *Symposium*, Phaedrus has clearly given much thought to the subject of *erôs* (177a5−c4) and is also well versed in the poets (177a6−b1); we are perhaps to understand that he has ransacked them looking for encomia of *erôs* in order to prepare his own. Certainly, his speech, with its opening quotations of Hesiod and nearly half of it given over to the stories of Alcestis, who was willing to die in her husband's stead, Orpheus, and Achilles, looks exactly like his speech of complaint which

Eryximachus had paraphrased immediately before; this, then, like Apollodorus's whole account, is no "unrehearsed" performance.[1] We may compare his rehearsal in the *Phaedrus* of the speech by Lysias; Phaedrus likes performing (*epideiknusthai*) and does not like to leave anything to chance. Citations of the great poetry and mythology of the past may be clearly appropriate in the sympotic setting, but they also establish at the outset the fact that it is indeed the poets who fashion and transmit society's common notions, which—as Socrates is there to remind us—it is the duty of "lovers of wisdom" to interrogate. Phaedrus's speech may in fact be seen as an extended version in prose of a common poetic structure: an assertion of some general truth (as the speaker sees it), followed by exempla drawn from myth to illustrate that truth.

Exempla, of course, like larger-scale mythic narratives, can be made to show anything and can be manipulated as the speaker wishes; there is no such thing as an unalterable, "canonical" account. Thus, in the spirit of literary problem solving which was to become a standard feature of the symposia of the learned, Phaedrus (not unlike the pedantic scholars of later antiquity) adduces reasons to believe that Aeschylus was "talking nonsense" in making Achilles the lover (*erastês*) rather than the beloved (*erômenos*) of Patroclus. So too, his very idiosyncratic version of the story of Orpheus, whose trip to the Underworld was unsuccessful because the gods deemed him soft "because he was a lyre-player" (179d4–5), reflects the kind of jesting approach to inherited stories which could be amply illustrated from ancient sympotic literature of all periods.

All three of Phaedrus's exempla illustrate the flexibility of inherited stories. That Alcestis's willingness to die in her husband's stead is a paradigm of the power of *erôs* to induce self-sacrifice is at least not the most obvious interpretation, given the usual presentation of that emotion (above, pp. 16–17); that she surpassed her parents-in-law "in *philia* because of her *erôs*" (179c1–2) merely calls attention

---

[1] Note Pausanias's pointed conclusion to *his* speech: "This, Phaedrus, is my contribution on Eros. It's the best I can do on the spur of the moment" (185c2–3).

to the manipulation.[2] *Philia* and *erôs* may, of course, coexist, even in a marriage, and Pausanias will introduce us (in a pederastic context) to "strong friendships (*philiai*) and partnerships, which . . . *erôs* most of all tends to implant in us" (182c3–4), but Phaedrus's lack of explanation or theorizing, a feature in which he differs markedly from Pausanias, who follows him, induces skepticism. Moreover, why an action which would have led to Alcestis's permanent separation from her husband, Admetus (contrast Achilles' deliberate death), should be an act of *erôs* is left quite unclear. That Achilles had the courage "not only to die for his lover Patroclus but also in addition to him" (180a1) is at best a loose reading of the *Iliad*, and one seemingly more concerned with verbal wit than with truth; that the gods transported Achilles to the Islands of the Blessed because it was his lover he had avenged is a simple rhetorical fiction invented for the purposes of the argument.

It is indeed the very profusion of mythic voices, which ingenuity can multiply without limit, which hinders the advancement of understanding. Story A can be used to trump story B, but where does this actually get us? A very similar thing is true of poetic citation. Phaedrus's citational practice is hardly unparalleled in omitting two "nonessential" verses from his opening quotation of Hesiod's *Theogony*, but we ought at least to ask whether Plato wants us to recall that the quotation continues " . . . Eros, most beautiful among immortal gods, limb-looser, who subdues the mind (*noos*) in the breast and the sensible planning (*epiphrôn boulê*) of all gods and all mortal men" (*Theogony* 120–22). No doubt these verses too could be turned to encomiastic use, but they are perhaps less appropriate to a philosophical gathering of men allegedly devoted precisely to *noos*; the omission of these verses advertises the simple, rather unsophisticated manipulations of Phaedrus's speech. The Platonic Socrates himself, of course, is not slow elsewhere to find confirmation of his views in the great poets of the past, but poetic citation

---

[2] So too at Xenophon, *Symposium* 8.3, adduced as a parallel by Dover (1978) 52, we are clearly dealing with some kind of in-joke: Socrates speaks: "Nikeratos, as I hear it, loves (*erôn*) his wife and is loved back (*anteratai*)."

alone is no substitute for argument; Phaedrus counts authorities rather than asking about their authority. "Lacking, it would seem, in native force of intellect, Phaedrus relies upon authority and tradition" is Bury's rather stern judgment;[3] later examples of self-parody from the other guests may, however, incline us to give Phaedrus some benefit of the doubt (cf. above, p. 10).

Philosophical gatherings, including symposia, no doubt regularly subjected the apparently high-minded words of poets to critical examination (cf., e.g., *Republic* 1.331e−34b on Simonides), but there can be a very Socratic objection to the practice as a whole. In the *Protagoras*, after a lengthy discussion of another poem of Simonides, Socrates observes: "Gatherings such as ours . . . have no need of other voices or of poets, whom one cannot question concerning their meaning; when they are brought into discussions, some say that the poet means one thing, others say another, and people discuss a matter which they have no way of determining" (347e). Socrates' point (whether ironically intended or not) is that the poet is not present, and one cannot interrogate a recited quotation, any more than a written text (cf. *Phaedrus* 275d−e); in fact, the *Symposium* is to offer us major contributions from two practicing poets who are indeed present to defend themselves, if necessary. Nevertheless, Phaedrus's witty contribution allows us to see that the citation of poetic and mythical exempla of a traditional kind cannot take us beyond mere assertion. We may be tempted to extrapolate from his two principal examples (Alcestis and Achilles), both of whom had been dramatized on the tragic stage, to the nonphilosophical status of mythic drama as a whole.

At the heart of Phaedrus's speech lies a claim that *erôs* induces a proper sense of shame in regard to shameful acts and an ambitious striving (*philotimia*) to perform honorable deeds. An *erastês* would do anything rather than be seen doing something disgraceful by his *erômenos*, and vice versa. If this principle were applied to the composition of an army, it would sweep all before it. *Erôs* can, therefore, make up for "natural" deficiencies of, say, courage (179a7−b3) in

---

[3] Bury (1932) xxv.

those who fall into its power. It is important that, at the beginning of the series of speeches, it is the positive social and moral effects of *erôs* which are foregrounded, for this is to be a principal focus in the dialogue as a whole.

Phaedrus, of course, is operating entirely with very traditional (even archaising) notions of "shameful," "honorable," and "virtue" (*aretê*), as is clear from his appeal to Homer and soldiery, though the bravery of its citizen-soldiers was indeed crucial to the survival of any ancient city; the tradition of laudatory speeches at funerals, such as that which Thucydides places in Pericles' mouth in book 2 of the *History*, shows the continuing potency of these inherited concepts. Nevertheless, within the context of a Socratic dialogue, we may regard it as important that Phaedrus makes no effort to argue that *erôs* would help a lover to distinguish the shameful from the honorable—what these are is silently assumed to be part of the unexamined conglomerate of knowledge which every member of society possesses, whether or not he is to fall under the spell of *erôs*. As such, Phaedrus foreshadows a central element (and deficiency) of Pausanias's erotic program; Pausanias's observation that actions (drinking, singing, having a discussion, loving) are not of themselves honorable or shameful, as everything depends on how they are done, may be likewise intended to cap Phaedrus's simplistic assertiveness (180e4–81a6). Moreover, Alcibiades, who otherwise feels no shame at all, will offer an example of a beloved who does indeed feel shame in front of his lover; this proves to be a counterexample, however, as it is a species of "striving after [political] honor" (*philotimia*) which pulls him away from that lover (216a–b).[4] Where Phaedrus claims that the beloved is the last person whom a lover would wish to see him break ranks or desert (179a3–40), Alcibiades must confess to "running away" from where he knows he should be—with Socrates (216b5). *Erôs*, as commonly understood, is not apparently enough.

[4] Cf. Xenophon, *Memorabilia* 1.2.14–48 for a parallel account of Alcibiades' *philotimia*, which shares several features with Alcibiades' account in the *Symposium*.

2 | Pausanias

A bout Pausanias we know very little; Plato presents him and Agathon as an *erastês-erômenos* couple in the *Protagoras* (315d6–e3),
set at least a decade and a half before the *Symposium*, and this long-
standing relationship (cf. 193b7) is clearly central to the speech
which we will hear from him. In the *Protagoras* he is presented as listening avidly to the famous sophist Prodicus of Ceos, and there is perhaps some amused reflection of this influence in Pausanias's opening
insistence on distinguishing forms of *erôs*, for linguistic differentiation,
the "proper use of words," was a prominent interest of Prodicus.

Although Pausanias did not, in the fictional symposium, follow
immediately after Phaedrus (180c1–2), he does so in the *Symposium*
which Plato provides for his guests/readers. We should, therefore,
ask how Pausanias caps Phaedrus's encomium. The beginning would
seem to be auspicious, for whereas Phaedrus had (apparently) taken
it for granted that we all know what *erôs* is, Pausanias begins by
making a distinction between two kinds of *erôs*. This "clever" move
introduces Pausanias's role as the group's *nomothetês*, "layer down of
laws." We may compare how Socrates, speaking in the guise of a
lover pretending not to be in love with a boy he hopes to win over,
caps Lysias's speech on the same subject:

> In everything, my boy, there is one starting-point for anyone
> who is going to deliberate successfully: he must know what
> it is he is deliberating about, or he will inevitably miss every-
> thing. Most people are unaware that they do not know what
> each thing really is. So they fail to reach agreement about it
> at the beginning of their enquiry, assuming that they know
> what it is, and having proceeded on this basis they pay the
> penalty one would expect: they agree neither with them-
> selves nor with each other. . . . [L]et us establish an agreed
> definition of love, about what sort of thing it is and what
> power it possesses, and look at this as our point of reference
> while we make our enquiry whether it brings advantage or

harm. Well then, that love is some sort of desire is clear to everyone. . . . (*Phaedrus* 237b7–d4; trans. Rowe)

In fact, however, Pausanias's initial concern is not with what *erôs* is (a subject which he never reaches), but with what kind of *erôs* deserves encomium. That there is "good" and "bad" *erôs* is an idea crucial to both Pausanias and Eryximachus, whereas for the second group of speakers (Aristophanes, Agathon, Socrates/Diotima) *erôs* is *tout court* a good thing.

Pausanias establishes two kinds of *erôs*: the older, Eros Ouranios, is the companion of Aphrodite Ourania, who was born—as her name indicates—"from the foam (*aphros*)" in the sea where Ouranos's genitals, severed by his son Kronos, fell (cf. Hesiod, *Theogony* 188–202), whereas the younger, Eros Pandemos (of all the people), works together with Aphrodite Pandemos, the child of Zeus and Dione (cf., e.g., *Iliad* 5.370–430). For the purposes of his *epideixis* Pausanias has systematized, or sharpened, an opposition between two epithets of Aphrodite with cult associations. "Ourania" may be applied to any god, with the meaning "heavenly," though the Greeks knew the Great Mother of various Eastern religions as "Aphrodite Ourania," and Ourania was certainly a known cult title of Aphrodite at Athens (cf. Pausanias 1.19.2).[5] The Athenians too had a long-standing cult of Aphrodite Pandemos[6] and, just as the epithet Ourania offered scope for interpretation, so did Pandemos, which Pausanias, with sympotic ingenuity, turns from a political epithet probably celebrating the goddess's link to "the whole people" to one suggesting the promiscuity of a love "available to all." Having hypothesized a divine structure, Pausanias, like an archaic poet describing the divine order of the world, moves to the spheres of activity and control of each god: different gods must operate in different spheres. Here, however, he perhaps loses the clarity of Hesiod, whose

[5] Cf. Hdt. 1.105, 131; Pausanias 1.14.7. On Aphrodite Ourania, see also Ferrari (2002) 107–11. Pausanias 9.16.3 describes three "ancient" wooden statues of Aphrodite at Thebes—"Ourania," "Pandemos," and "Apostrophia" (Rejector, i.e., "of unlawful desire and impious actions").

[6] Cf. Pirenne-Delforge (1988); Stafford (2000) 121–29.

Theogony was the principal Greek text on the divine structure, for he shifts from the idea of different spheres of activity to the moral evaluation of individual activities. No activity (*praxis*), he argues (181a), is honorable or shameful of itself, but everything depends on how it is done. We ought, therefore, to not praise just Eros, but only the Eros "which encourages us to love honorably" (181a6).[7]

Pausanias's simple dualistic model, matched by an equally simplistic moral model of "good" and "bad," raises a number of questions, though the rhetorical agenda which informs them will soon become clear enough. The fact that, as an activity, *erôs* is per se morally neutral but can have good and bad manifestations ought not to mean that it is a different *erôs* which makes us act in different ways, any more than different Dionysuses make us drink "honorably" and "shamefully." Moreover, we have already seen that the evidence of cult names on which Pausanias bases the plurality of Aphrodite and Eros is not to be pushed too hard. In Xenophon's *Symposium*, Socrates, presumably responding to this argument, accepts that there are different cult practices, but keeps an open mind as to the conclusions to be drawn from that: "Whether Aphrodite is single or double, 'Ourania' and 'Pandemos,' I don't know; Zeus, who always seems to remain the same, has many titles" (Xenophon, *Symposium* 8.9). The Xenophontic Socrates thus already calls attention to a potential weakness in Pausanias's argument, one which is still fought over by modern historians and philosophers of religion.

For Pausanias, the *erôs* which works with Aphrodite Pandemos (herself the product of an adulterous union) is promiscuous in the sense that it operates without social and educational distinctions—Pausanias is nothing if not a self-proclaimed elitist—and it aims merely at sexual gratification, being *erôs* for the body rather than the soul (181b3–4). All *erôs* for women is of this kind. We may be tempted to put this observation down to Pausanias's long-standing relationship with Agathon—the primary audience for the whole speech—but in fact this rejection of heterosexuality (and, at least implicitly, of female homosexuality) is of a piece with the main body of the

[7] The Greek may also be translated as "which honorably encourages us to love."

speech, which is to be concerned with *erôs* as a force for the transmission of civic *aretê*; as women are "by definition" excluded from such *aretê*, they must also be excluded from "good" *erôs*. More broadly, of course, the intimate link which Plato is constructing between *erôs* and philosophy means that homosexual relations must be privileged in any paradigm, even a mistaken one, of the getting of wisdom, and this Platonic tradition was to have a long history in antiquity. A Platonizing pederast in Plutarch makes similar use of a distinction between true *erôs*, which is pederastic and has higher purposes, and "desire" (*epithumia*), which aims at pleasure and enjoyment (*Amatorius* 750c–e); on this view, so it is alleged, men no more feel true *erôs* for women than flies do for milk or bees for honey. The same character also recounts that when someone complained to Aristippus of Cyrene (late fourth–early third century) that the courtesan Lais, whose sexual services he was presumably purchasing, did not love (*philein*) him, Aristippus replied that he did not imagine that wine and fish loved him either, yet he derived pleasure from both.

Aphrodite Ourania, on the other hand, has no mother and therefore she and the corresponding *erôs* have nothing to do with heterosexuality.[8] As the goddess is older than Aphrodite Pandemos (as Kronos is older than Zeus), so she and those inspired by her have the characteristics of the old—they have put youthful outrages (*hybris*) behind them (181c4) and are interested in the mind rather than the body. The "sophistical" equivocation—X is "younger" than Y and therefore "young," whereas Y is "mature"—is as much at home in the play of the symposium as will be Pausanias's joke that in societies such as Elis and Boeotia, where people are no good at speaking, it is always honorable for boys to grant their favors to lovers, as this spares the lovers having to make speeches of persuasion (182b1–6). The disavowal of *hybris*, however—a term which, in sexual contexts, is regularly used in connection with rape or

---

[8] The playfulness of Pausanias's distinction may be seen from the fact that Pindar describes how the temple prostitutes of Corinth "frequently soar in their minds towards Aphrodite, the heavenly (*ourania*) mother of loves" (fr. 122.3–5 Maehler).

other forms of sexual attention which bring dishonor—and the praise for relationships which begin when the younger man's beard is starting to grow and which then last, as shared partnerships, throughout life clearly take Pausanias's relationship with the listening Agathon as an ideal model (181d4−5; cf. Aristophanes' words about Pausanias and Agathon at 193b7−8).[9] Finally, in the section devoted to the two types of *erôs* Pausanias introduces the subject which, apparently, is closest to his heart: the conditions under which *erômenoi* should indulge (*charizesthai*, show *charis* to) their lovers (182a1−6). His "heavenly *erôs*" thus also involves physical relief for the lover, but only under specific circumstances.

The second part of Pausanias's speech, for which the first has prepared, is a normative description of the practice of pederasty in Athens, which he acknowledges to be complex (*poikilos*), "not easy to grasp" (182b1), and which would seem to an outside observer to be riddled with inconsistencies; pederasty is indeed another activity which is neither honorable nor shameful of itself, but the evaluation of it is entirely dependent on how it is done (183d4−8). Many modern scholars would grant Pausanias at least this: same-sex relations of all kinds in Athens were indeed a problematic area of social anxiety, where custom and convention (*nomos*) dictated a much more mixed set of attitudes than the law (also, in Greek, *nomos*) defined.[10] Put baldly, Pausanias argues that pederastic practice in Athens is broadly divisible into two kinds (another of his rhetorical dualities): good practice and bad. In both kinds, both *erastês* and *erômenos* may be characterized by different attitudes and purposes, but it is again the conditions under which sexual favors may honorably be granted to which the argument leads.

[9] So too 183e5−6 (Pausanias), "the lover of a good character lasts throughout life, as he is fused together with something long-lasting," looks forward to Aristophanes' speech and clearly suggests Pausanias and Agathon again. At Xenophon, *Symposium* 8.2 Socrates explicitly refers to young men who are simultaneously *erômenoi* and (just developing) *erastai*.

[10] Cf. Cohen (1991) chapter 7, citing much earlier bibliography. The subject cannot be pursued in detail here. For different views on the historical origins of Greek "didactic" pederasty (a subject only of marginal interest for the *Symposium*), cf. Dover (1988) 115−34.

Good Athenian pederasty for Pausanias is of the following kind. The older *erastês* expresses his love and pursues his object openly, rather than secretly; he loves the younger man's soul rather than his body, and wishes to make the younger man better, by making him "wise and good," by "contributing to understanding (*phronêsis*) and the rest of *aretê*" (184d7–e1); beyond this education and the friendship which attends it he offers the young man nothing (such as money, power, and so on). The *erômenos* similarly acts out of a wish to be made "wise and good" and does not sell himself for money, power, or other advantage; he will not grant sexual favors easily or quickly, for there must be time to see that the lover really is of the right sort and not merely interested in physical gratification. Bad pederasty is everything else, or any relationship in which one of these conditions is not fulfilled. According to Pausanias, social custom in terms of encouragement for the *erastês* in his pursuit and the physical and moral checks which are placed upon the behavior of younger men support this complex situation of approval and disapprobation.

As an encomium, this is at least strange, for the speech as a whole certainly suggests that the "good *erôs*," which activates the "good pederasty," is much rarer than its opposite. Moreover, and this is something which will become important in Socrates' speech, *erôs* is here felt by the older *erastês*, whereas the younger *erômenos* (lit. he who is loved) will feel at most "affection" (*philia*; cf. 182c4);[11] despite this, the results of the *erôs* are entirely centered upon the younger man's improvement. If we were to ask what the (honorable) *erastês* derives from his *erôs*, then there seem to be two possible answers: a not explicitly expressed emotional satisfaction that he is doing good by helping a young citizen toward virtue and, second, physical satisfaction ("favors"; note especially 184d4–5).

Pausanias might have been a witness on the side of those who believe that Plato was familiar with the idea of an *erôs* which is generous and directed to the good of the beloved, as well as with the

[11] There is a nice illustration at Xenophon, *Hiero* 1.37, "A private citizen has immediate evidence that, whenever his beloved (*erômenos*) yields, he is offering the favor (*charizesthai*) out of affection (*philôn*). . . ."

selfish, appetitive *erôs* of mainstream Greek opinion,[12] were it not for the obvious gravitational center of Pausanias's concerns, namely, the sexual satisfaction of the *erastês*. A cynic might be forgiven for thinking that the good *erastês* derives little more from his *erôs* than does the bad one. What, moreover, we might be tempted to ask, can *erastai* do for young men that a good father cannot do, for the paternal model is clearly analogous to, though of course also crucially different from, the pederastic one. Thus, in the pederastic verse of Theognis, the poet gives advice about conduct "as a father to his son" (v. 1049), and the Socrates of the *Republic* outlaws the "mania" of sexual pleasure for *erastai* who love properly: "although a lover can (if he can persuade his boyfriend to let him) kiss and spend time with and touch his boyfriend, as he would his son—which is to say, for honorable reasons—still his relationship with anyone he cares for will basically be such that he never gives the impression that there is more to it than that" (*Rep.* 3.403b5–c1; trans. Waterfield). The fraught ambiguities of this passage of the *Republic* (just what kind of physical contact *is* envisaged?) are a powerful indication of the anxieties that surround sexual behavior in an educational context.

Crucial for Pausanias's program, then, is an implicit acknowledgment of the universal and awkward reality (awkward for everyone except Socrates, at least) of physical desire requiring physical release, and this program must be seen as at least a rhetorical strategy for channeling and controlling that brute fact. Whether such a program, particularly as regards sexual relations, was realizable in practice was something which need not have concerned Pausanias or his fellow guests. To an outside observer (or a modern reader), indeed, it may seem that such a program might be merely a fine mask for the indulgence of sexual drives, and a fragment of fourth-century comedy seems already to reflect such attitudes:

> What are you saying? Do you expect me to believe that a lover (*erastês*) who loves a boy in his prime is a lover of his character and is truly sober-minded (*sôphrôn*), with no interest in what he sees? I believe this no more than I believe that

[12] The debate may be pursued through Rist (1964) and Osborne (1994).

a poor man who constantly pesters the rich doesn't want something. (Amphis fr. 15 Kassel-Austin)

The fact that an outside observer may see things differently does not, of course, mean that the practitioners themselves do not sincerely believe in the reality of the fine ideals they espouse or that these ideals are not realized in practice. On the other hand, it is at least worth asking how many members of Pausanias's immediate audience we are to imagine as "believing" his account of Athenian practice: Agathon's guests and Plato's readers, of course, knew that all sympotic discourse was a mixture of the "serious" and the "playful." The speech by the nonlover in the *Phaedrus* (above, p. 33) shows how easily Pausanias's arguments can be flipped over in the service of a different rhetoric.

Despite this, much modern interest in Pausanias's speech has been, unsurprisingly, focused upon the question of how accurate a picture of Athenian social customs it affords. Some of the detail of his speech does indeed seem to be confirmed from other sources,[13] and Plato creates internal consistency through Alcibiades' similar account of the rules of the game in which he thought he was engaged; we must be careful, moreover, to distinguish Pausanias's description of alleged Athenian practice from his proposed ideal and idealistic pattern of philosophic pederasty (184c7–85c1). What are, however, perhaps more important than the historicity of the social practice which Pausanias depicts are the awkward questions of real social relations which his presentation elides. It will, for example, be left to Alcibiades to fill in for us one of the many areas which Pausanias leaves unexplored: the almost inevitable fact that *erômenoi* will exploit the universal need of all lovers for sexual release, and the dependence which that need brings, as a weapon in the game of education. Unfortunately for Alcibiades, Socrates was the exception that proved the rule, but the rule is a fatal flaw in Pausanias's rosy picture. The lover (unless he be Socrates) will thus inevitably say what the beloved wishes to hear because of the "favors" upon which the former is so dependent. As an orator or politician also claims to make an audience better, but must play to (*charizesthai*) and flatter

[13] The classic study here is Dover (1978).

(*kolakeuein*) the crowd if he is to be successful (cf. *Gorgias* 502d–3a), so the lover's desire for a successful conclusion to his pursuit will determine the character of any exchange with the beloved.[14] Sexual favors, then, are not something given out of gratitude for betterment or wisdom gained, but are determinative of the nature of that wisdom.

As for the *erômenos*, how will he become better with respect to virtue? No answer is given, but the obvious inference—and one which corresponds to ancient notions of teaching and of the relationship between master and pupil or father and son—is that he will become like the *erastês*, who is "a decent person" (*chrêstos*, 183d7). This last word had also been used by Phaedrus—"I cannot myself say that there is a greater good for a young man than a *chrêstos* lover and for a lover than a (*chrêstos*) boyfriend" (178c4–5)—and though Pausanias has been more explicit than Phaedrus as to what constitutes such "decency," his speech represents in fact little advancement of clarity in this regard; it is at least reasonable to infer that Phaedrus too was only praising *erôs* of an honorable, nonmercenary kind. The principal difference between the accounts of Phaedrus and Pausanias lies in the explicitly didactic role of the *erastês* in the latter. Whereas in Phaedrus's speech, *erôs* will make someone behave "rightly," for Pausanias *erôs* is a force which makes not its object, but its object's beloved wiser and better.

The possible objections to Pausanias's model are easy enough to see. If the *erastês* is to make a young man "better and wiser," then—on a conventional model of teaching—he himself must be a wise man, as Alcibiades realized that Socrates manifestly was; but in what this wisdom might consist is never examined. Phaedrus had laid stress upon traditional military virtues such as courage, whereas the most flattering inference to be drawn from Pausanias's speech is that, broadly speaking, it is "citizenship" in which the older man will mold the younger, who himself will one day become a "good *erastês*." A less flattering interpretation would see Pausanias entirely preoccupied with an ever-recurring round of sexual practice, so that it is

[14] An excellent discussion is in Nightingale (1995) 47–59.

simply the didactic circle of how *erômenoi* are taught to be *erastai* which is of concern to him; in this latter case, "wisdom" and "virtue" will simply be part of the self-serving vocabulary with which a particular subgroup of society justifies its practices. On the more favorable interpretation, however, Pausanias is describing a particular form of the nonprofessional transmission of cultural knowledge common to all societies, but one which was a source of special anxiety (for some) in the latter part of the fifth century and the early part of the fourth because of the rise of professional educators, particularly those whom we, somewhat inaccurately, group together as "the sophists." This new kind of professional educator could be represented, as happens for example in Aristophanes' *Clouds*, as dismantling the traditional, largely family-based, structures by which one generation instructed another and society was preserved and protected. Thus, in the *Protagoras*, Plato makes Protagoras undertake to make men "good citizens" (319a), as Hippias too offers to make men "better with respect to *aretê*" (*Hippias Maior* 283c), and it is this "citizenship" which lies at the heart of Protagoras's great speech in his dialogue; Socrates then questions Protagoras about *how* he will make his students better and in what the *aretê* which he professes to teach consists. Pausanias's model is traditional, not innovative, but Socrates' cross-examination of Protagoras's claims shows us what kind of an examination might lie in wait for Pausanias's unreflective notions.

That Pausanias is indeed thinking of (an ill-defined) civic virtue is also suggested by the political frame of his pederastic program. Whereas Phaedrus drew solely on poetic myth, Pausanias's principal exhibits are the greatest heroes of Athenian democratic myth, the tyrant-slayers Harmodius and Aristogeiton (celebrated also in drinking songs performed at elite Athenian symposia),[15] and his pattern of pederasty is allegedly rejected in tyrannies and nondemocratic states. This political rhetoric is particularly important, as it is likely

[15] For the love of Harmodius and Aristogeiton adduced as beneficial to Athens, cf. esp. Aeschines 1.132, where they are immediately followed by Achilles and Patroclus; Wohl (1999) 355–60. That this love "put an end to the rule" of the Athenian tyrants (182c6–7) is certainly an exaggeration; cf. Thucydides 6.53–58.

that the almost ritualized type of homosexual practice which Pausanias describes was perceived or could be represented as an elite, upper-class activity carried on by those with too much time on their hands and an attachment to democracy which was always at least open to question (cf. above, p. 7). In his apologetic picture of Socrates, Xenophon shows him reproving the oligarch Critias for his designs on the pretty Euthydemus, and the language precisely appeals to a sense of social class:

> When [Socrates] realized that Critias was in love with Euthydemus and was trying to seduce him like those devoted to physical sexual pleasure, he tried to stop him by saying that it was not worthy of a free man (*aneleutheron*) and not fitting for a gentleman (*kaloskagathos*) to plead with his beloved, whose good opinion he wished to have, and implore him like a beggar, asking him to grant something which was, moreover, no good thing. (Xenophon, *Memorabilia* 1.2.29)

Plato's defense of Socrates' role in the love life of Alcibiades, another high-profile associate of Socrates of dubious democratic credentials, will be rather more artful. Nevertheless, it seems unlikely that the "willing slavery" of the *erastês*, as described by Pausanias (183a–b), would be thought to be "something very excellent" (183b4) by anyone outside a reasonably restricted, and self-absorbed, circle in which the coded language of such behavior was fully understood. That such behavior was "of great value to the city" (185b6) would probably have come as news to many ordinary Athenians; what the Platonic Socrates, whose real-life model the democratic city had executed in part for "corrupting young men," thought of it, Alcibiades' speech will clearly demonstrate.

3 | Eryximachus

The speeches of Eryximachus and Aristophanes offer universally applicable models of how *erôs* functions in the world, drawn, respectively, from science and mythical storytelling. If both the humor and irritating suggestiveness of Aristophanes' double-people theory has long been recognized, criticism has, on the whole, been less kind to Eryximachus, a doctor and close friend of Phaedrus (177a–d; cf. *Protagoras* 315c2–3). The doctor's much less generally accessible speech has been taken to be just a parody of the jargon-ridden "grand unifying theories" of fifth-century science and medicine.[16] In other words, the critical assumption has been that Eryximachus takes himself perfectly seriously (and is therefore more than a little ridiculous), whereas Aristophanes and Agathon, at least, and perhaps also Pausanias, are conscious of the sympotic atmosphere to which their discourses must be adapted. Such a way of reading seems, however, overly harsh.

Eryximachus's *epideixis* is a kind of sampler of medical theory and discourse, and we know that doctors did indeed make public (and absolutely serious) displays of their wares and their skills, medical and rhetorical, in this way.[17] Eryximachus's performance, however, is festive and self-knowing in its very overfullness (cf. 188e1–3); in this it resembles the deliberate over-the-topness of Agathon's verbal and rhythmical style, which wittily exaggerates and distorts what seem to have been genuine features of the real Agathon's poetic style (below, pp. 73–77). Of course, there is also both humor at Eryximachus's precise pedantry (note the way he gives the full source for his tragic quotation at 177a3) and parody of the medical profession and its theorizing. Plato seems to have had no time for the exaggerated claims of medicine, which had little in common with what he saw as the true pursuit of understanding (philosophy),[18] and we are clearly meant to sympathize with Aristophanes' obvious amusement at Eryximachus's performance. Nevertheless, pleasure and amusement are precisely the ends at which such sympotic *logoi* should aim, and Eryximachus not only gives us both but also enters into the spirit of things with his mock-solemn prescrip-

[16] Criticism of such theories was itself a standard rhetorical move of some doctors; cf., e.g., Hippocrates, *On the Nature of Man* 1, *On Nature* 1.

[17] Cf., e.g., Jouanna (1984); Lloyd (1979) 86–91; Thomas (2000) chapter 8; Thomas (2003).

[18] The best place to start is *Republic* 3.403d–10b.

tion for curing hiccups (185d1–e2); although doctors were indeed interested in such things,[19] we are perhaps to understand that the cures which this learned doctor prescribes were as universally familiar then as they are now. His apparently labored interpretation of a dark utterance of Heraclitus (187a3–b2) is, moreover, of a piece with the familiar half-serious problem solving and critical discussion of the symposium.

The sixth and fifth centuries BC were an extraordinarily productive period of scientific observation and speculation all over the Greek world (the inquiry into nature). As part of this revolution, medical theory and practice flourished in the second half of the fifth century and later, and some at least of our large collection of classical medical texts (the Hippocratic corpus) will date from this period. Much in Eryximachus's speech finds close parallels and analogies in these texts. It is perhaps not very surprising that he adopts the "scientific" analysis of the fundamental qualities of cold and hot, dry and wet (186d7, 188a3–4),[20] but there are passages where the Hippocratic resonance of the argument is strongly marked. Thus, for example, his definition of the art of medicine— "Medicine, to put it in a nutshell, is the science (*epistêmê*) of the erotics of the body with regard to repletion (*plêsmonê*) and emptying (*kenôsis*), and the man who can distinguish the fair and the shameful love in these matters is the most doctorly person" (186c5–d1)—like much else in his speech, finds close echoes in two parallel passages from what are all but certainly early Hippocratic treatises:

Emptying cures repletion and repletion emptying, as rest cures weariness. To put it briefly, opposites are the cures of opposites, and medicine is subtraction and addition, subtraction of what is in excess, addition of what is in deficiency. The man who best does this is the best doctor, and the one who falls shortest of this falls shortest of the art also. (Hippocrates, *On Breaths* 1)

[19] Cf., e.g., Hippocrates, *Aphorisms* 6.13.
[20] Cf. Lloyd (1964).

> Emptying cures all diseases produced by repletion, and repletion cures all which arise from emptying; those which arise from exercise are cured by rest, as those which arise from idleness are cured by exercise. . . . [T]he doctor must relax what is tense and make tense the relaxed. (Hippocrates, *On the Nature of Man* 9)

So too, Eryximachus shares with the author of the Hippocratic *On Regimen* an interest both in Heraclitus (*Regimen* 1.5; 187a) and in the musical harmony of highs and lows as an analogy to the creation of harmony in the body (*Regimen* 1.8; 187b–d). In this Hippocratic treatise the musical material is part of a theory of how all the arts (*technai*) are like the nature of man, starting from seercraft, *mantikê*, to which Eryximachus too addresses himself at 188b6–d3 (*Regimen* 1.11–24). The arguments of the two doctors are quite different, but Eryximachus's all-encompassing claims, which explicitly embrace medicine (in all of its areas, including dietetics, the effects of climate, the seasons, and so on), music, and seercraft and which reflect a similar kind of (what we would see as) polymathy, do share the structuring strategy of *On Regimen*. The Hippocratic flavor of the speech is indeed important to its proper appreciation. More broadly, some of the basic ideas of the speech—mixture, the harmonization of opposites, the alternation of excess and deficiency—are among the most staple tropes of medicine and science of many different intellectual traditions.

Eryximachus takes up Pausanias's duality of *erôs*, but extends it to the whole natural and divine world, an insight which he has gained from his medical art.[21] The encomium therefore becomes (unsurprisingly) in part an encomium of medicine, which is the art which knows how to use and implant *erôs* (186c7, d4), and of its practitioners (of whom Eryximachus himself is the prime ex-

---

[21] Modern readers have been divided over the form and merits of Eryximachus's argument. I have found Rowe (1999) of most help, although the account that follows differs from his in certain respects; further bibliography may be traced through Rowe (1999) and, for earlier treatments, Martin (1931) 87–92.

ample), just as Pausanias's speech is in part an encomium of one particular kind of *erôs*, of which Pausanias and Agathon are the chief example. "Good love" is the desires of the healthy part of any body, "bad love" those of the unhealthy. The healthy and the sick will, for example, both want and require different diets (cf. *On Ancient Medicine* 3), and the doctor must know how to "promote the interests" (again, *charizesthai*) of the healthy part and show no favor (*acharistein*) to the unhealthy (186c2–5); the result of his ministrations will be the reign of "good *erôs*" and thus good health. More broadly, an unhealthy body will want unhealthy things: thus, for example, a body which is too cold (i.e., in which "cold" has encroached on the space of "warm" and thus caused unhealthy imbalance) will want more cold and reject the warmth which it needs for health. A good doctor can reconcile the two opposed qualities (186d1–5), can make them "love each other."

Eryximachus's speech, therefore, does not merely use the familiar pre-Socratic idea of the necessity to harmonize opposites, but also foreshadows Diotima's crucial idea that *erôs* must be for something which you do not have already: the cold cannot "love" cold, only warm. So too, the skilled musician reconciles opposites (high and low notes) which were formerly at variance with each other, in order to produce a harmonious concord by implanting "*erôs* and agreement" in them; by a definition parallel to that for medicine, music is "the science of erotics concerned with harmony and rhythm" (187c4–5).[22] Behind the parallelism of the two arts lies Apollo, both father of the founder of medicine, Asclepius (186e2; cf. 190e, 197a6–7), and divine musician: Apollo promotes harmony both in the body and in music (cf. *Cratylus* 405c–6a). Although—so Eryximachus seems to say—anyone would be able to recognize (*diagignôskein*) "the erotic element" in harmony and rhythm per se, i.e., realize that all harmony and rhythm depend upon an *erôs* of contrasting tones and speeds, nevertheless a "good practitioner" is needed for the ac-

---

[22] The nature of the "bad *erôs*" in the case of music remains rather unclear: many commentators see Eryximachus tangled up in the rigid scheme he has proposed.

tual composition and teaching of music (187c5–d4); in the same way, it is obvious that the health of the body has to do with *erôs*, but it requires a "good practitioner" to know how to diagnose (*diagignôskein*) the fair and the shameful *erôs* and produce good health through erotics.

Eryximachus parts company with Pausanias in not rejecting entirely from his musical theory "the common love," here associated with the Muse Polymnia, whose name might be half-seriously interpreted as "music for the many." The expert must know how to apply it (as a doctor applies remedies), so that its undeniable physical pleasures may be enjoyed while any risk of "wantonness" (*akolasia*), presumably arising from addictive overindulgence, is avoided (187e1–3).[23] Plato here seems to put in his doctor's mouth a version of his frequently expressed fear of the moral effects of music which plays to the crowd, which lacks the "good order" (*kosmos*) which should be the necessary aim of all psychological and medical therapy (cf. *Gorgias* 504a–c). Musical developments of the late fifth and fourth centuries did indeed, as Plato stresses in the *Laws*, break down traditional modes and harmonies and—or so conservatives complained—aimed merely at the baser pleasure and arousal of the audience; it is such music (and contemporary criticism of it) which is mocked by Aristophanes in the *Women at the Thesmophoria*, where Agathon is a principal practitioner of the new art. With the musician's double knowledge, Eryximachus compares the doctor's need to know about "desires concerned with the art of cooking," an art which Plato elsewhere (cf. *Gorgias* 462d–63c) treats as a kind of sham medicine and which here functions as the popular counterpart of medicine, one aiming, like popular music, at pleasure (rather than health). Doctors must know about cooking so that their patients can enjoy food but remain healthy (187e4–6); the deleterious effects of elaborate "arty" cooking, no less than those of elaborate "arty" music, are a recurrent theme of Plato's writing.[24]

[23] Foucault (1985) 51 is pithy but a bit misleading: "it . . . rests with [doctors] to prescribe . . . how to have an orgasm without any resulting ill effects."

[24] Cf., e.g., *Republic* 3.404d–e, where music and cooking are again explicitly linked.

With the role of *erôs* in seercraft, Eryximachus might be thought to have overreached the usefulness of his model, though *mantikê*, like medicine, is also concerned with the interpretation of signs and the move from the visible to the invisible (cf., again, *On Regimen* 1.12).[25] More problematic, within Eryximachus's repetitive model, is astronomy, "the science of erotics concerned with the movements of the stars and the seasons of the years" (188b5−6), for it is hard in this case to see how any human practitioner could do anything to correct imbalances, and here indeed Eryximachus stays purely at the level of theoretical knowledge rather than practical intervention. In one of those turns, however, which occur throughout the work, a new and apparently rather inconsequential idea is now introduced which is to assume great significance later.

According to Eryximachus, *erôs* regulates the relations between gods and men, and it is the seer's role to keep this relationship healthy by the proper use of sacrifices and prayers; at base, presumably, the idea is that all prayers and sacrifices are about human desires, or *erôtes*, just as divine attitudes toward humans could also be seen as a matter of desire. The specialist is again an erotic expert: "seercraft is a practitioner of friendship between gods and men through its knowledge of human erotics, insofar as they aim at right and piety" (188d1−3). When things go wrong, in other words, when the disorderly Love governs relations, impiety occurs, and it is necessary for the seer to restore the proper balance, as a doctor restores the body. We may be reminded of Sophocles' *Oedipus Rex* in which Oedipus has plainly "gratified the disorderly Love . . . with respect to parents"; the state is diseased as a result and, as in the first book of the *Iliad*, a seer must be summoned in an attempt to restore the normal balance between man and god. That *erôs* mediates between man and god is something that we will next hear from Diotima (202e3−3a7), and in a context which will encourage us to take it very seriously.

---

[25] Medicine and seercraft as analogous, but also opposed, crafts are powerfully dramatized through the medical imagery of Sophocles' *Oedipus Rex*; Oedipus and Teiresias embody the two very different kinds of knowledge.

4 | Aristophanes

Aristophanes' speech is in some ways the most surprising of all the encomia of the god.[26] Plutarch regarded the speech as a "comedy thrust into the symposium" (*Moralia* 710c), but at first glance we seem a world away from the Aristophanes of the surviving comedies. Plato's character indeed calls Eros "the most human-friendly (*philanthrôpotatos*) of gods" (189d1), a term which the chorus of Aristophanes' *Peace* uses in an appeal to Hermes for his help (*Peace* 392), but that does not seem very much to go on. Remarkably absent, for example, is any sign of (even mild) personal satire; the mockery of named Athenian citizens (*onomasti kômôdein*) was perhaps the single feature of the comedy of Aristophanes' day most often remarked upon, by both opponents and supporters, and although we would not expect any harsh mockery within the well-ordered context of the symposium (cf. above, p. 12), the absence of even much worth the name of jesting is noteworthy. Certain motifs do indeed find analogies in Aristophanic comedy (cf. below), but most of the humor on show is of a rather different kind.

Aristophanes' first words after Eryximachus's speech—the "desire of the orderly part of the body" (189a3−4)—teasingly parody the doctor's language and thought, and Eryximachus then tells him not to play the fool (like, we might think, the clown Philip in Xenophon's *Symposium*), which leads to an Aristophanic equivocation (189b6−7) between *geloion* (humorous) and *katagelaston* (ridiculous);[27] here perhaps is a glimpse of the Aristophanes we know. The

---

[26] For a full-length study of Aristophanes' contribution to the *Symposium*, cf. Ludwig (2002). Reckford (1974) is a sympathetic reading of Aristophanes' speech as "Aristophanic."

[27] At 189b1, Eryximachus warns Aristophanes not to say anything *geloion*, by which he means "mocking (with the sole intention of raising a laugh)," as Eryximachus has (probably rightly) taken 189a1−6 and as was a standard elite interpretation of the whole nature of comedy (*Republic* 10.606c is important here). Aristophanes replies that to say something *geloion*, which he uses in the sense of "amusing," would be entirely appropriate both to the situation and to himself—his fear rather is that his speech itself will deserve nothing but mockery.

speech which follows, however, is comedy of a kind not normally associated with the Old Attic Comedy of Aristophanes. Toward its end, Aristophanes himself protests (too much?) that his words are not to be misinterpreted: "Eryximachus must not protest and make a mockery (*kômôdôn*) of my speech by saying that I'm talking about Pausanias and Agathon. . . . what I'm saying applies to everyone, men and women . . ." (193b6–c3). Certainly, some gentle teasing continues: the opening of the speech picks up, almost indeed paraphrases, the conclusion of Eryximachus's; the god himself becomes a doctor (189d1–2; cf. 193d5) whose skills hold out hopes of the greatest happiness (in contrast to what mortal doctors can do for us?), and Aristophanes undertakes to teach his audience the nature (*phusis*) of man and what has happened to it, lessons which (again) we would expect to hear from a doctor. So too, when Aristophanes talks of men finding sexual "satisfaction" (lit. filling; *plêsmonê*, 191c6), we are presumably to remember Eryximachus's definition of medicine (above, p. 55) and draw the amused conclusion that Aristophanes is learned in medical lore; for males, of course, sexual satisfaction is more like an emptying (*kenôsis*) than a filling. The description of Apollo's healing (190e2–91a5), which likens the god to a cobbler or leatherworker, would presumably be found unflattering by any contemporary surgeon; surgery is, however, likened to the art of the cobbler in the Hippocratic treatise *On Regimen* (1.15), which we have already seen to throw light upon Eryximachus's speech. It may, therefore, be that Aristophanes is again finding comic material in the scientific ideas and texts which Eryximachus reveres. Nevertheless, such teasing is of the gentlest sort, and nothing in the body of the speech remotely resembles comic invective.

There is, of course, much more to Aristophanic comedy than invective, and we may even wish to see the speech of the Platonic Aristophanes as a reflection of what seems to have been the innovative style of Aristophanes' comedy with respect to some of his contemporaries; we know that not all Old Comedy, and certainly not all of Aristophanes, was harshly invective in the mold of, say, Aristophanes' own *Knights*. Nevertheless, any reading of Aristophanes' speech must ask why Plato has given a speech of this form to the comic poet to whom in the *Apology* (19c2–6) and elsewhere he ascribes part of the responsibility for popular prejudice against and misunderstanding of Socrates. Aristophanes is not, however, necessarily out of place at Agathon's gathering, either socially or politically. It can be plausibly argued that the political stance of Aristophanes, and of Old Comedy generally, was not just conservative but in fact openly hostile to the more radical democrats and their leaders; the association between Aristophanes and "Socrates' set" is, despite the satire of Socrates in the *Clouds*, by no means implausible.

Aristophanes' myth may be seen as a radical revision of the "battles of Titans, Giants, and centaurs, the fictions of men of old," which Xenophanes had banned from the well-conducted symposium (fr.1.21–2, above pp. 6–7); certainly Aristophanes' moral (193d3–5) shows the exemplary piety which Xenophanes had demanded. Previously, begins Aristophanes, we were not as we are now, but we were double creatures, resembling perhaps two modern humans standing back-to-back with their limbs stretched out in parallel: everyone had two faces (on either side of a single head), two sets of genitals, four legs and four arms, and moved quickly by tumbling along. There were three kinds of "doubles": male, female, and mixed. These powerful ancestors of ours got out of hand, like Ephialtes and Otus in Homer (*Odyssey* 11.305–20), and tried to storm heaven to attack the gods. Zeus eventually decided to split all these creatures down the middle into two, at right angles to the direction of their faces. The result was two-legged, two-armed creatures (male and female); each being's face was then turned through 180 degrees so it now faced that plane of itself which had been cut, and this plane was healed and molded by Apollo into a chest and stomach, though he left the navel "as a reminder of the ancient suffering" (191a4–5). These "halves" went around looking for "their other halves," and when they found them they locked together in an embrace as they tried to reunite; in their desperation they ate nothing and so died. Out of pity, Zeus now completed the surgery by turning the genitals also through 180 degrees (i.e., to where they are now), so that when a man and a woman embraced, their genitals would meet and through procreation the race would continue;

so too, when man embraced man there would be physical satisfaction (*plêsmonê*) which would enable the men to get back to work (Zeus's plan being largely motivated by a desire for men to be useful to the gods).[28]

Although this narrative of the double-people is set far in the past, it also explains both our present situation and the varieties of human desire and practice. We all spend our lives searching for our lost half, whether that be of the same or a different gender, and the kind of sex we enjoy is determined by the gender of that missing half; sex is, in fact, part of our pursuit, or as Aristophanes puts it, "*erôs* is the name for the desire and pursuit of the whole" (192e10). If an original couple is lucky enough to find each other again, the result is amazing:

> It's impossible to describe the affection, warmth, and love they feel for each other; it's hardly an exaggeration to say that they don't want to spend even a moment apart. These are the people who form unbroken lifelong relationships together, for all that they couldn't say what they wanted from each other. I mean, it's impossible to believe that it's their sex-life which does this—that sex is the reason they're each so eager and happy to be in the other's company. They obviously have some other objective, which their minds can't formulate; they only glimpse what it is and articulate it in vague terms.
>
> Imagine that Hephaestus came with his tools and stood over them as they were lying together, and asked, "What is it that you humans want from each other?" And when they were unable to reply, suppose he asked instead, "Do you want to be so thoroughly together that you're never at any time apart? If that's want you want, I'd be glad to weld you together, to fuse you into a single person, instead of being two separate people, so that during your lifetime as a single person the two of you share a single life, and then, when you

---

[28] Aristophanes is apparently thinking only of the possibility of front-to-front (intercrural) sex between two men; as his model is entirely nonhierarchical (cf. below); penetrative anal sex, in which one partner was seen as "active" and the other "passive," would be out of place.

die, you die as a single person, not as two separate people, and you share a single death there in Hades. Think about it: is this your hearts' desire? If this happened to you, would it bring you happiness?" It's obvious that none of them would refuse this offer; we'd find them all accepting it. There wouldn't be the slightest doubt in any of their minds that what Hephaestus had said was what they'd been wanting all along, to be joined and fused with the one they love, to be one instead of two. (192b7–e9)

We must, however, behave properly toward the gods, or Zeus will split us again, as he had threatened at the time of the original partition (190d4–6). It is Eros, however, who is able to grant males the best possible conclusion to their search in the present circumstances, namely, a congenial *erômenos* (193c7–8); the final part of Aristophanes' speech concentrates almost entirely upon male homosexual relations. Eros also offers us the hope for the future that, by restoring us to our original wholeness, he will make us "blessed and happy" (*makarios* and *eudaimôn*, 193d5). If we only understood the blessings which Eros can bestow, we would never cease praising him and establishing cults of him.

We may well smile as we recognize something of ourselves and our own sexual pursuits in the comedy of Aristophanes' half-people, and certain features do remind us of comic scenes and motifs. Both Aristophanes' *Peace* and *Birds* concern threats to the Olympian order and—more specifically—the uncertainty of the gods when confronted by the threat of the double-creatures, and their fear at losing honors and sacrifices (190c1–6) is reminiscent of their plight in the *Birds*, cut off from earth by the new foundation of Cloud-cuckooland and hence starved of the sacrifices they previously enjoyed (*Birds* 1515–20; cf. *Wealth* 1112–19). So too, the difficulty which Zeus has in coming up with a scheme to confront the danger is clearly a comic contrast to the traditional ease and speed of divine thought. That successful politicians, to a man, "showed affection for (*philousi*) men and enjoyed lying locked in embrace with them" when they were young (191e7–92a1) is a polite version of the frequent comic jest that all politicians were "rent boys" in their youth (e.g., *Knights* 878–80), just as adulterers (*moichoi*; cf. 191d6–e2) also litter the extant plays. The allusion to the fate of the Arcadians (193a3), the homely images of hopping on one leg in a popular game (*askôliazontes*, here in Zeus's mouth), of cutting apples and eggs, of flatfish,[29] and of a drawstring purse, all suggest not merely the topical reference and exuberant everyday imagery of Aristophanes' extant plays, but also that mixture of the mythical and the contemporary which must have been a hallmark of the mythological burlesque which flourished on the Attic comic stage in Plato's day, if not in Aristophanes'. More broadly, it is easy enough to see how Apollo's banausic skill in cobbling humans might be thought to come from the same kind of comic imagination in which, for example, War makes a salad out of the Greek states (*Peace* 236–88). Although evidence for speaking of one's beloved as "my other half" is largely later than Plato, it is also tempting to believe that Aristophanes' narrative is to be understood as an example of a very familiar aspect of the technique of Aristophanic comedy, namely, the literalization of metaphorical language (as, for example, when "weighing up" poetry becomes a matter of real weighing in the *Frogs*).

The logic of this narrative is not to be pushed any harder than the logic of real Aristophanic narratives (Dicaeopolis's private peace in *Acharnians*, the sex strike in *Lysistrata*, and so on), although its closest extant analogues are rather in the world of Aesopic fable and popular storytelling than in Old Comedy.[30] The logic is that of the etiological "just-so" story: a one-time event in the past (such as a young elephant's encounter with a crocodile) has universal consequences in the present (all elephants have long trunks). Thus, for example, in Hesiod the gods once created the beautiful but destructive woman Pandora and gave her to Epimetheus, but all women are now like her. Slightly different, because it deals in ab-

[29] Wilson (1982) 161–63 argues for an explicit allusion here to Aristophanes, *Lysistrata* 115–16.

[30] Cf. Dover (1966) which should be consulted for other analogues to this narrative.

stracts, but clearly related to such narratives is Socrates' remark at *Phaedo* 60b–c on how pleasure and pain always go together "as though they shared one head": "I think that, if Aesop had noted this, he would have composed a story (*mythos*) about how god wished to reconcile them and stop them warring, and when he found that he couldn't, he joined their heads together." Very close to such an Aesopic etiology will be Diotima's story that explains the mixed nature of Eros, the son of Resource and Poverty; in this too Socrates will be made to cap all the speeches which have gone before.

Whereas Eryximachus's speech had covered the workings of the whole cosmos, Aristophanes stays firmly in the world of human desire; nevertheless, we are clearly to read these speeches together as opposed (cf. 193d7), or perhaps complementary, ways of seeking to understand the world, ways which, without investing too much in the actual labels, we might call the scientific and the mythic. Whereas the former depends on privileged knowledge only available to an expert, and to some extent upon explanations of a subtlety which reinforces the very need for such expertise, the latter appeals to "facts" allegedly observable by anyone who wishes to construct an explanation for those facts. That the Athens of the late fifth and early fourth centuries was a ferment of such competing explanations, a society as multivocal as the *Symposium* itself, is a familiar fact of intellectual history. In the *Clouds*, Aristophanes himself had dramatized part of this ferment. Of particular interest is *Clouds* 365–411, in which the comic Socrates explains, with the help of analogies drawn from the behavior of the stupid Strepsiades' stomach, that the clouds and "Whirl," not Zeus, are responsible for natural phenomena such as rain, thunder, and lightning; this is a low comic version of the same kind of "scientific" explanation which Eryximachus gives for disturbed weather patterns in 188a–b. Although Eryximachus's speech certainly did not eliminate the role of gods, other than Eros, in human affairs (188c–d), it certainly tended—as scientific and medical explanations must[31]—to diminish their impor-

---

[31] A classic text here is the opening chapters of the Hippocratic *On the Sacred Disease*.

tance (as does, with comic ridiculousness, the Socrates of the *Clouds*), whereas the Platonic Aristophanes (like Diotima in myth-telling mode) makes his Olympians very real indeed.

The faultlines of Aristophanes' story are not limited to its just-so logic. Thus, for example, birth and childhood are not easily accommodated to the idea of our original doubleness (where is a baby's "other half"?), but this problem is elided in the consideration of pederasty (191e6–92b5): men whose other half was male are, apparently, *erômenoi* when young and *erastai* when they have grown up. If they are lucky enough to find their other half, the relationship, as that of Pausanias and Agathon, will persist into the adulthood of the younger partner. Nevertheless, Aristophanes' speech does offer something which no speaker before him has done, namely, a definition of *erôs*—the pursuit of wholeness (192e10)—and a description of what it feels like to be "in love." Many modern readers of Plato have felt that this definition and description correspond to a real aspect of "being in love," namely, the sense that the loved one somehow fills an absence in the lover, makes him or her "whole"; moreover, the mythic fantasy of original union is as good a way, probably better, of accounting for the mystery of why any individual loves another than any attempt to list the reasons to a higher standard of proof. Very few Platonic texts have become the basis for successful rock-operas, but Aristophanes' speech can claim this distinction. *Hedwig and the Angry Inch*, a stage show (1998) and subsequently a film (2001) by John Cameron Mitchell and Stephen Trask, tells the story of a transsexual rock singer from East Berlin in search of her other half after a botched sex-change operation. The key song of the show, "The Origin of Love," sets Aristophanes' speech, sometimes almost verbatim, to music, and the splitting of the double-people is made analogous, inter alia, to Eve's separation from Adam and to the partition of Berlin. There can be few more unexpected testimonies to the continuing popular power of the Platonic-Aristophanic myth.[32]

[32] For the influence of this myth, cf. also below, pp. 130–32. One potential "other half" who confronts Hedwig is called "Tommy Gnosis" (i.e., Knowledge); knowledge was certainly the object of Socrates' search.

It is not just the description of our universal search which has proved influential and productive. Aristophanes' claim that the souls of a reunited couple want something from each other, something which is not just sex, that "the emotional storm of physical passion . . . contains within itself a metaphysical element . . . an aspiration that transcends the limit of the human condition and that cannot possibly be satisfied in the way that hunger and thirst can be satisfied,"[33] is clearly important for the later stages of the *Symposium* and has struck a powerful chord in more than one modern reader; the relief which sex (even sex with one's other half) offers is, as we know only too well, a temporary one, and our persistent need for, and persistent dissatisfaction with, this second-best solution is an uncomfortable fact about the human condition. Aristophanes' lovers find it difficult to know or articulate what exactly it is that they want (192c3–d2), but readily assent to Hephaestus's suggestion that it is complete fusion. Socrates' speech will suggest a rather different answer.

As for the importance of this speech for our view of antiquity, Aristophanes' extraordinary fable has become a classic text in the tracing of a shift from the hierarchical structures of pederasty as described by Pausanias to a more symmetrical and reciprocal pattern of erotic relations, both homo- and heterosexual, observable both in real social patterns and in the literature of later antiquity.[34] Certainly, the travails and travels of the separated couples of the ancient novel, two young people equally beautiful and equally virtuous, might well fit Aristophanes' definition and narrative of *erôs* (cf. below, pp. 127–28). Socrates will make Diotima reject, or at least radically revise, the central proposition of Aristophanes' myth (205d10–6a1), but the attractiveness of that proposition is apparent in the ancient and modern reception it has received. It may be the case that lovers would not in fact answer Hephaestus as Aristophanes (rather dis-

[33] Kahn (1996) 268.

[34] Cf., e.g., Konstan (1994); further discussion and a bibliography are in Hunter (1996); and cf. further below, pp. 127–28. Much modern discussion starts from Foucault (1985), e.g., 232–33.

ingenuously) claims they would,[35] except in the first afterglow of passion, but love precisely promotes such fancies and unrealizable wishes, and no one is going to demand that lovers in bed together give reasoned and thought-out answers to important questions; just how hard then ought we to push the Aristophanic model?

The glorification of narcissism and self-regard might seem to be the most potent dangers of the Aristophanic model, though the comic poet shows us how "love of self" and "love of other" are intimately connected. The preceding speeches have also conditioned us to ask other questions of this fable. The story has a simple and virtuous moral—we should be pious toward the gods—but what will each of us derive if we are lucky enough to find our other half? According to Aristophanes, Eros is responsible for "the greatest benefits by leading us toward what is our own (*oikeion*)" (193d2–3), and if he consents to "heal" us by making us whole again, we will be "blessed and fortunate." The inculcation of piety may be a conventionally praiseworthy aim, though it seems unlikely that Aristophanes' story would pass the censorship which Socrates elsewhere seeks to impose upon stories which do not rightly portray the gods (*Republic* 2.377a–3.392c). Be that as it may, we must ask in what this happiness consists, and the answer can only be some kind of blissful trance in which there is no obvious role for the intellect or improvement of the individual (who will of course no longer exist)[36] or the body politic at large, except insofar as the practice of piety is helpful to the state. Socrates and Diotima will show us (again) that an encomium of *erôs* must explain the positive nature of what *erôs* does for us, and this Aristophanes has singularly failed to do. A Platonic answer to Hephaestus would stress that what every lover should want is help in the ascent toward knowledge. We cannot fail

[35] Cf. Rowe's (1998) note on 192e6–9. Rowe suggests that the whole idea of "doubleness" derives from sexual intercourse, in which two human beings, with four arms and four legs, get as close to each other as possible. Thus, the Spice Girls' song of 1996 entitled "Two Become One" was, unlike the similar motifs in *Hedwig and the Angry Inch*, probably not indebted (consciously) to Plato.

[36] Cf. Aristotle, *Politics* 2.1262b11–14.

to recall here the stress in the *Symposium* upon the "loneliness" of Socrates: as he stands absorbed in thought or refuses to play Alcibiades' game, there is no sign that he is desperately searching for another human being. His search, as Diotima will suggest, is of a rather different kind.

Aristophanic plays regularly conclude with the celebration of the heroes, now "blessed and happy," in a world apparently improved; *makarios* and *eudaimôn* are words often applied to successful comic heroes as the play draws to a close.[37] We might think of the end of *Acharnians*, of *Lysistrata*, or of *Women in Assembly*, in which the whole state is treated to a banquet after relinquishing power to the women. Particularly in the so-called parabases of his plays, in which the chorus addresses the audience directly, Aristophanes claimed to address seriously the serious issues of the day; for Plato, however, comedies may be "feel-good" performances in which awkward questions both about the plot of the play and its general civic subject are simply swept aside in a tide of communal jollity. Aristophanes' last two extant plays, the *Women in Assembly* of 392 and the *Wealth* of 388, are both excellent examples of this.[38] So too is the Platonic Aristophanes' performance in the *Symposium*: inventive, witty, appealing, naggingly suggestive, but at heart utterly empty. We finish "blessed and happy" but none the wiser, not unlike, in fact, old Demos (the people) in Aristophanes' *Knights*, "blessedly restored to his ancient state" (v. 1387; cf. 193d5), but in fact no further forward. Restoration of previous happiness is indeed a prime motif of Aristophanic plots (cf. *Acharnians*, *Peace*, *Lysistrata*), and with this hope for the future Aristophanes leaves us smiling. Like all of the encomiasts, therefore, the Platonic Aristophanes has put *erôs* to the service of his own project (though we—and he?—would still like to know the identity of Aristophanes' own other half). Unlike, however, the Silenus Socrates and the dialogues which describe him (cf. below, p. 100), and unlike Diotima's model of birth

[37] Cf. Macleod (1981).

[38] According to the conventional chronology, Plato would not have been a resident in Athens in these years, but such plays may well have been influential on his ideas of what comedy was.

and pregnancy (cf. below, pp. 82–83), opening up Aristophanes' double-people brings diminution and loss, not revelation. Happiness, *eudaimonia*, is crucial (204e6–5a3), but we should be searching not for the lost half of ourselves, but inside what we already have.

5 | Agathon

The speech which forces out Socrates' ironic formula for encomium (above p. 36) is the coruscating performance of the tragic poet (and host of the party) Agathon. In the *Protagoras* Socrates describes the adolescent Agathon as "of a fine (*kaloskagathos*) nature and of very fine (*kalos*) looks" (315d8–e1) and, though probably around thirty in 416 BC, he still plays the role of beautiful object of desire at his own symposium. His speech, moreover, depicts Eros as an idealized version of the "model *erômenos*," namely, Agathon himself in his prime —young, beautiful, soft, and creative—and in part the embodiment of all the cardinal virtues (as prescribed in the *Rhetoric to Alexander*, above p. 35).[39] Even by the highly rhetorical standards of the *Symposium*, however, Agathon's speech is marked by an explicit self-consciousness with its own technique and structure ("There is one correct method of praise in all situations . . . ," 195a1) and by many forms of word- and sound-play (puns, equivocations, antithesis, assonance, rhyme, and so on), which often take the place of, while simultaneously advertising the absence of, anything that could be described as "convincing argument."

In the *Gorgias*, Socrates asserts, and Callicles agrees, that tragedy is just a kind of "flattery," which aims at the pleasurable gratification of the audience (502b), and the Agathon of the *Symposium* is precisely designed as an illustration of that view. Agathon's frequent references to the "evidence" or "proof" (often, "powerful evidence") for his assertions (195b1, d6, e1; 196a5, e4) again show a self-conscious reveling in the ingenuity (and emptiness) of argumentation. The demonstration that *erôs*, a force which normally makes one lose all sense

---

[39] Stokes (1986) 114–82 offers the fullest available attempt to take Agathon's speech seriously.

of self-control, is perfectly *sôphrôn* (sensible, controlled, moderate, chaste) may serve as a nice example of Agathon's pleasure in paradox: "It is agreed that *sôphrosunê* is ruling over (*kratein*) pleasures and desires, and that no pleasure is stronger (*kreittôn*) than Eros. If the pleasures are weaker, they would be ruled (*kratein*) by Eros, and he will rule (*kratein*), and if Eros rules over pleasures and desires he will be extraordinarily *sôphrôn*" (196c4−8). The argument for Eros's wisdom (*sophia*) is also worth following, both for itself and also because "wisdom" is a matter very close to the hearts of Plato and his Socrates.

Traditionally in Greek culture *sophia* is "skill" and may be applied as readily to a purely manual facility (e.g., ship making) as to an intellectual talent. It is a standard word in earlier poetry (notably Pindar) for "[skilled] poetry," and it was with this sense that Socrates had already teased Agathon (175e1−6; cf. Aristodemus at 174c7); this is where Agathon unsurprisingly starts his account, even though this is not the expected *sophia* of an encomium. The "argument" runs as follows (196d6−e6): Eros is so *sophos* a *poiêtês* (lit. maker, but a standard term for "poet") that he can make (*poiei*) other people into poets; the evidence adduced for this is a famous quotation from a lost play of Euripides: "Eros instructs a poet, even if he was without the Muses beforehand" (fr. 663 Nauck). As one cannot teach what one does not know, this demonstrates that Eros is a skilled *poiêtês* in every branch of *poiêsis* (lit. making, of which poetry is a particular instance) concerned with music. As for the *poiêsis* (making) of all living creatures, this too is obviously the work of "Love's wisdom"; the thought will be that (1) *erôs* is responsible for all sexual activity and procreation (197a2−3; cf., e.g., Euripides, *Hippolytus* 447−50; Lucretius, *DRN* 1.1−20), and (2) this will be "wise," because through this, nature continues and prospers (cf. Aristophanes' narrative at 191c5−6). It will be left to Diotima to offer an explanation for the slippages which such language allows (205a−c on the broad and narrow senses of *poiêsis*). Next, any "practitioner of an art" who has been taught by Love will be "glorious and conspicuous,"[40]

[40] "Conspicuous" (*phanos*; lit. bright, shining) is chosen to recall Socrates' description of Agathon's "shining" *sophia* at 175e4.

but any who is not touched by Love will remain obscure. This might look like a rather weak extension from the case of poetry and of Agathon himself to all craftsmen, but it picks up Eryximachus's thesis about *erôs* and the arts, as the language of "practitioners" (*dêmiourgoi*) and the pointed "do we not know?" (197a4), that is, now that Eryximachus has told us, demonstrate.

For Eryximachus, a skilled practitioner, such as a doctor, had to know about the *erôtika* relevant to his subject; Agathon merely extrapolates from this the view that a good practitioner, i.e., one who succeeds in restoring the proper *erôs*, must in doing so be guided by Eros. It will, therefore, follow that the gods who invented the various arts (which are all concerned with *erôs*) were also guided by Eros, though this then slides into a different, though related, claim that this guiding *erôs* was a "love of beauty" (197b4–5), because the arts are beautiful/fine (*kala*) for both gods and men. Just before his brilliant peroration and at the conclusion of a remarkably slippery argument, then, Agathon incidentally introduces what will become a crucial idea: *erôs* must be *erôs* for something. In his claim that it is "very obviously *erôs* for beauty—for there is no *erôs* for ugliness" (197b4–5), he will prove both right and wrong, in ways which we cannot yet suspect.

In the closing section of the speech, an almost untranslatable incantation of rhythmical phrases, a beautiful sound signifying nothing, brings Greek prose as close to metrical poetry as it ever got:[41]

> Eros draws insularity out of us and pours familiarity into us,
> by causing the formation of all shared gatherings like ours,
> by taking the lead in festal, choral, sacrificial rites. He dispenses mildness and dismisses wildness; he is unsparing of goodwill and unsharing of ill-will. He is gracious and gentle; adored by the wise, admired by the gods; craved when absent, prized when present. Hedonism, luxury, and sensualism, delight, desire, and eroticism—these are his children. He looks after the good and overlooks the bad. In adversity and uncertainty, for passion and discussion, there is no bet-

---

[41] To the commentators add Dover (1997) 169–71.

ter captain or shipmate or guardian deity; for the whole of heaven and the whole of earth, he is matchless and peerless as governor and guide. (197d1–e3)

Socrates says that the speech reminded him of the famous Sicilian rhetorician Gorgias, and though Gorgias's prose style does not really share the rhythmical character of Agathon's peroration, we can see what Socrates means. It may in fact be that Agathon's conclusion, "Let this speech of mine be dedicated to the god, one which partakes both of play (*paidia*) and of moderate earnestness" (197e6–8), is an explicit allusion to (and rewriting of) the conclusion of Gorgias's famous *Encomium of Helen*, " . . . this speech which is an encomium of Helen and a plaything (*paignion*) of mine." The *Encomium of Helen* is a prominent example of epideictic rhetoric on paradoxical subjects in which what is on display is the cleverness of the speaker (above, pp. 35–36); such works notoriously have nothing to do with truth, and as such this closing allusion to Gorgias, if such it is, is one more way in which Plato guides our interpretation of Agathon's speech. Even without this allusion, however, the association between Agathon and Gorgias is clear. Gorgias's *Encomium* is characterized by many of the verbal features which we have noted in Agathon's speech—rhyme, assonance, wordplay, and so on—and a central section on the incantatory, magical power of words, which are "carriers on of pleasure, carriers off of pain" (*Encomium* 10), would find no better illustration than the Platonic Agathon's peroration. A famous fragment of Gorgias's *Funeral Oration* gives some idea of what lies behind Socrates' comparison:

> What did these men lack that men should have? And what did they have that men should lack? May what I say be what I sought to say, and what I sought to say what I ought to say—free from the wrath of gods, far from the envy of men. They had the virtue that is instilled by gods, and the mortality that is inborn in men . . . schooling themselves into what was most needed: might of hand and rightness of plan, thinking through the one and acting out the other; succour-

ers of the unfairly unfortunate, punishers of the unfairly fortunate; assertive when advantage called, yielding when pro-
priety forbade; restraining hastiness of hand with prudence
of plan; confronting outrage with outrage, orderliness with
order; fearless in the face of the fearless, feared themselves
in the midst of things to be feared; in testimony to which
they raised trophies over their enemies: for themselves, dedications; for Zeus, consecrations; strangers neither to the fire
of battle in the blood, nor chaste loves, nor armour-clad
strife, nor beauty-loving peace. . . . Dead though they be,
our longing for them dies not; but deathless in bodies not
deathless, it lives, though they live not. (Gorgias fr. 6 Diels–
Kranz; trans. T. Cole)

In view, however, of Plato's persistent association of Gorgias with a
persuasive rhetoric which pays no regard to truth, Socrates' charged
comparison of Agathon to Gorgias looks to the (lack of) substance
of what was said, as well as to the style in which it was expressed.

Of the real Agathon's tragedies only the scantiest fragments survive; a high proportion of these is indeed marked by verbal wit (including rhyme and assonance) and smartness, but the body of evidence is extremely small.[42] Of greater interest for present purposes
is the fact that Agathon appears as a character already in the *Women
at the Thesmophoria* of Aristophanes (411 BC). In this play Euripides
asks his fellow tragedian to infiltrate an all-female gathering to
speak on his behalf; Agathon would be able to do this because he is
"fair-faced, white, shaven, of feminine voice, soft, and lovely to be-
hold" (*Thesm.* 191−92). We recognize here a comic version of the
same characteristics which are highlighted in the *Symposium.* So
too, in the *Women at the Thesmophoria* both the comic Agathon and
his servant are characterized by a self-consciousness about tragic art,
which is revealed in a series of craft metaphors applied to poetic
composition (*Thesm.* 52−57, 67−69; cf. Plato, *Phaedrus* 234e) and in

[42] The standard edition is volume 1 of B. Snell and R. Kannicht (eds.), *Tragico-
rum Graecorum Fragmenta*, 2d ed. (Göttingen: 1986) 155−68.

a rather confused set of principles about the relationship between a poet and his productions which the comic Agathon enunciates:

> I wear my clothes along with my mentality. A man who is a poet must adopt habits that match the plays he's committed to composing. For example, if one is writing plays about women, one's body must participate in their habits. . . . If you're writing about men, your body has what it takes already; but when it's a question of something we don't possess, then it must be captured by imitation. (Aristophanes, *Women at the Thesmophoria* 148–56; trans. Sommerstein)

After this concept of mimetic adaptation, the comic Agathon seems to argue for an intrinsic relationship between a poet's appearance (and his clothes) and the poetry he writes:

> Phrynichus . . . was an attractive (*kalos*) man and he also wore attractive clothes, and that's why his plays were attractive too. One just can't help creating work that reflects one's own nature. (Aristophanes, *Women at the Thesmophoria* 164–67; trans. Sommerstein)

The Platonic Agathon's speech and his picture of Eros are clear projections of himself (as Plato portrays him), and there is thus a shared substrate ("you write as you are" or vice versa) to the portrayals of the tragedian in both Plato and Aristophanes. Unfortunately, only more information than we currently possess about the real Agathon and his works would allow us to understand what really lies behind these representations. On the verbal level, the Agathon of Aristophanes' play, "Agathon of the beautiful language (*kalliepês*)" (v. 49), and his servant are characterized by redundancy, rhyme, assonance, and antithesis (note especially vv. 146–47),[43] and again we see how the Aristophanic and Platonic representations share important characteristics. The Aristophanic portrayal can, moreover, help to explain the extravagance of the Platonic character's speech. Agathon

---

[43] Aristophanes also drew attention to Agathon's fondness for antithesis in another play (the *Second Thesmophoriazousai*); cf. fr. 341 Kassel-Austin.

is playing not just to an elite and highly literate audience, but to one containing a poet who has already parodied him in fairly strong terms; he disarms such criticism by going "beyond parody" in a deliberately over-the-top challenge to conventional criticism. The winning self-knowledge thus revealed is perfectly at home in the looking glass of the symposium.

· 3 ·

The Love of Socrates

1 | Socrates

Socrates undertakes to speak "as suits me / on my own terms" (199b1), and his contribution does indeed fall into two modes familiar from other Platonic dialogues: question-and-answer, which reveals the answerer's ignorance, clears away misconceptions, and prepares for what is to follow, and, second, longer "didactic" speeches, first by Socrates and then by Diotima. In the progression from speech (Socrates) to dialectic (Socrates examining Agathon) to further dialectic (Diotima examining Socrates) and finally to Diotima's great speech of myth and metaphysics, Socrates' personal role becomes progressively less important. Although each successive speaker to some extent caps those who have preceded, only Socrates (and Diotima) address specific questions to the immediately preceding speaker: it is apparently truth, not rhetorical and performative effectiveness, which is now to be the central concern.

Socrates begins by praising Agathon's encomiastic strategy of first describing (*epideixai*) "what sort of thing *erôs* is" and only then "what it is responsible for" (199c2–6; cf. 195a1–3). "I very much admire that beginning," says Socrates, and we can see why: it is a

78

strategy which can be easily accommodated to one of the most familiar aspects of Socratic ethical discussions, namely, the quest for definitions of ethical terms. One cannot discuss what, say, "bravery" (as in the *Laches*) or even "beauty" (*to kalon*, as in the *Hippias Maior*), let alone "justice" (as in the *Republic*) can do for us, before having decided what these actually are. The Socratic dialogue in pursuit of definition is thus what a "true encomium" should look like. Plato himself shows this later in the *Symposium*. After Alcibiades' speech we are led to expect an encomium of Agathon by Socrates (223a1–2) and though our hopes are cut short by the revelers who burst in,[1] when Aristodemus restores our vision the following morning Agathon and Aristophanes are, with some difficulty, being driven by Socrates to accept that someone who is "by art" (*technê*) a tragic poet is also a comic poet, so that the same person knows how to (*epistasthai*) compose both forms of drama. Here we recognize an argument of typical Socratic form and apparent paradox (tragic and comic compositions were utterly separate arts in classical Athens), and it seems likely that we are indeed witnessing the promised encomium; it too will have started from a definition of terms and, like the dialectic between Agathon and Socrates which we do actually witness, may well have led Agathon to conclude that he knew nothing about a subject upon which he must have held views (201b11–12).

Socrates first gets Agathon to agree that *erôs* always involves *erôs* of something, whether this is stated explicitly or not: one can no more "be in love" without "being in love with something/someone" than one can be a "father" without being a "father of someone." The fact that *erôs* is relational is crucial for what follows, but Socrates' explanatory examples of "father" and "brother" also allow him to slip into talking about *erôs* in ways that we would more naturally associate with an *erastês*, that is, a person who embodies *erôs*, as a father embodies "fatherhood." Thus, for example, at 200a3 "*erôs* [rather than the *erastês*] desires," and the importance of the idea that

---

[1] We may be reminded of the revelry with which Attic comedy regularly ends and/or the "drunken young men" who form the chorus of many plays of New Comedy.

loving is always for the purpose of "permanent possession" is established through a series of personal examples (200c–e); we move seamlessly from "everyone who desires" (200e2) to "*erôs* is of certain things and indeed of those things which it lacks" (200e9–10). The payoff for this slide will come in the similarity, so close as to suggest an identification, of Socrates to *erôs*, as Diotima will depict the god. Second, Socrates' insistence upon the relational nature of *erôs* carries a criticism of the encomium which Agathon has just delivered: praise of *erôs* must inevitably consider also what is being loved, what the "*erôs* is of," whereas much of Agathon's speech, as indeed much of Phaedrus's, simply praised *erôs* and ascribed qualities to it, as though one could treat *erôs* in isolation from its working in the world. Even when poets describe what *erôs* is like, such descriptions normally have their starting points in particular erotic experiences and particular manifestations of *erôs* at work. It is worth adding that although Agathon had, almost in passing, noted that *erôs* must be "of beauty" rather than "for ugliness" (197b5), a view which Socrates describes as "reasonable enough" (201a8), ordinary Greek usage would have felt nothing odd about using *erôs* and its cognates with what would today be considered a *morally* disgraceful object. Just as the Greek for "beautiful" (*kalon*) is also the ordinary word for "honorable/morally right," so the word for "ugly" (*aischron*) also means "shameful/morally wrong"; for this reason, praise of *erôs* cannot shirk the question "*erôs* of what?"

Agathon is made to agree that *erôs* (we would find it easier to say "the lover") always "loves" and "desires [to have]" what this *erôs* is of, and this will necessarily involve the fact that this is something which *erôs*/the lover currently does not have. The modern reader may consider that Agathon should have held out against this proposition for rather longer than he does, but it is important to bear in mind (again) that *erôs* can be a much more powerful emotion than our "love"; it is a desire to possess, whether sexually or otherwise (cf. above, p. 16), and Agathon had used *erôs* and *epithumia* (desire) as virtual synonyms (197a7). When satisfied, as for example through sexual intercourse, *erôs* recurs, demanding to be satisfied again; we can therefore understand why it (as opposed to, say, *philia*) may be thought to carry an inevitable sense of lack and absence. An *erastês*, even a successful one, always "wants something."[2] The upshot is that Love cannot be at all as Agathon described it: if we (and the gods) love/desire beautiful and good (201c4–5) things, it follows that Love itself cannot be beautiful, as Agathon had claimed (201a–b). A rather labored Socratic pun—Agathon has made a big mistake about beauty, but spoke "beautifully" (201c1)—seals the criticism of a speech in which style had triumphed over content.

Socrates, we now discover to our great surprise, had a teacher in erotics, and a female one at that, Diotima ("honored of Zeus") from Mantinea in the Peloponnese, a place name which inevitably suggests *mantikê* (seercraft); certainly, Socrates' story of how she helped the Athenians in time of plague (201d3–5) recalls Eryximachus's account of seers as experts in a particular field of erotics who can restore a proper relationship between man and god (188b6–d2; cf. 202e2–3a8). There has been much discussion of the historicity of Diotima, though her role in the *Symposium* is obviously a fictitious one (she has even had an advance inkling of Aristophanes' speech, 205d10–e7), and we should no more wonder when she and Socrates used to meet than we should inquire when Er of Pamphylia told Socrates the story which concludes the *Republic*. It was common enough at symposia for the male guests to impersonate characters, including women, through the recitation of poetry, whether one's own or another's (the recitation of Sappho would be an interesting case),[3] and Socrates' gambit must be seen, in part, as appropriate to the setting in which he finds himself. As a female instructor of Socrates in matters of *erôs*, Diotima also has analogues in other Socratic literature, notably the famous *hetaira* and mistress of Pericles, Aspasia; another follower of Socrates contemporary with Plato, Aischines of Sphettos, wrote an influential work called *Aspasia* in which Socrates seems to have quoted this woman's views on *erôs* and *aretê*, and the Platonic Socrates himself claims Aspasia as

---

[2] It is possibly relevant that "to have" may have, in Greek as in English, a sexual sense.

[3] For verse imagined to be delivered by a woman, cf. also Theognis 257–60, 579–82; Alcaeus fr. 10 LP-Voigt.

his "schoolteacher in rhetoric" in the *Menexenus*, in which he recites by heart a funeral speech she allegedly composed for the Athenian war dead. More fundamentally, however, the procreative and reproductive model of philosophy which Diotima will espouse is appropriate to and reinforced by her femaleness.[4]

Socrates' performance very much enters into the inverted, Dionysiac world of the symposium. In apparently repeating all but verbatim the words of his instructor, we see him behaving like an Aristodemus or Apollodorus,[5] whose skill lies merely in the reproduction of remembered conversations; this is not the Socratic manner as we have come to know it from our acquaintance with Plato. So too, Socrates now places himself on the receiving end of a "Socratic" examination, or elenchus, followed by a long "Socratic" speech; the Platonic Socrates thus shows himself to be as self-aware about his normal procedures as had Agathon through his extravagant self-parody. The childlike naïveté of his alleged responses to Diotima may be seen as a reductio ad absurdum of the position of Socrates' interlocutors in some of Plato's most famous dialogues, who often contribute nothing themselves or find themselves agreeing, as modern readers often complain, to propositions and arguments to which they should never have unthinkingly assented.[6]

At the heart of Diotima's instruction will be the idea that *erôs* functions in allowing an individual to "give birth" to ideas and *logoi* with which (s)he is already pregnant; along the way, the individual requires a guide, who—as it were—turns Pausanias's ideal couple into a triangle. The crucial point, however, is that this is a model of philosophical advancement fundamentally different from Pausanias's, and one of which there will be no sign that Alcibiades, who is not present to hear Diotima, has any notion. For these characters, teaching, "becoming better," is a matter of "information transfer" from teacher/older man/lover (*erastês*) to pupil/younger man/beloved

---

[4] Halperin (1990) 113–51 is an important study of Diotima's female identity.

[5] The two introductions, 173e7 and 201d5–7, are very close.

[6] Plato elsewhere can joke about this "artificiality" of the dialogue form; cf. *Republic* 9.573d1.

(*erômenos*), whereas Diotima's concern is with the guided advancement by careful stages of an individual *erastês* (here radically redefined). As a woman, Diotima shows that the idea of an exchange of such intellectual information for sexual favors (*charizesthai*) is absurd, but the fact that she is a seer in touch with "mystic" knowledge allows Plato to have her instruct Socrates (cf. esp. 206b5–6, 207c5–6) as Socrates cannot and will not instruct Alcibiades or any other of his followers. The origin of Socrates' knowledge of the process of discovering about Beauty and the philosophic ascent is an unrepeatable "revelation"; the model of Socratic and Diotimic teaching is thus preserved.

Diotima herself is not "pregnant," though it might be thought that her mystic language is appropriate to the sex for whom pregnancy is a real physical possibility, and Socrates—in this sense at least—is not beautiful. Moreover, it is crucial that the central part of Diotima's revelation, which Socrates now passes on to his fellow guests, is precisely about the *process* by which men may climb the ladder of understanding toward the Form of Beauty (cf. below); at least in the speech which Socrates allows us to hear, Diotima does not herself take Socrates very far up that ladder. That Socrates (incredibly, if with the admirable politeness of a guest) presents himself as once upon a time as ignorant about *erôs* as Agathon is now, as emotionally but unreasoningly attached to "boyfriends" as any Athenian (211d5–8), and as entirely "unironic" and un-Socratic (as we are familiar with that mode from Plato's dialogues) reinforces the distancing effect of Diotima's intervention; it is not just the substance, but also the mode, of that intervention which will explain to us (but not to Alcibiades) Socrates' treatment of the politician.

Diotima begins by telling Socrates that although, as Agathon and he have agreed, Eros is not beautiful and good, neither is he ugly and bad; more than that, he cannot be a god, as all gods are "beautiful and blessed," and blessedness consists in the possession of good and beautiful things, whereas Eros precisely desires such things, because he lacks them (202c10–d3, picking up Agathon's words at 195a5–7). Eros is *between* beauty and ugliness, good and bad, god and human: he is a "great spirit" (*daimôn*), a member of a class which is neither mortal nor immortal. Though Diotima skillfully avoids naming the states which fall between beauty and ugliness and between good and bad, her (very Socratic) example of "correct opinion" as a halfway state between wisdom and ignorance (202a5–9) prepares the ground for the idea of the philosopher's quest and the philosophic *erôs*, which itself is "in the middle between wisdom and ignorance" (203e5); the halfway position can be viewed not as a permanent state, but as a stage in a progression toward a further and better state. For Diotima, the idea of "in-betweenness" is an elastic one: Eros exemplifies an intermediate state between immortal and mortal, but also literally shuttles "between" gods and men as a kind of messenger or intermediary, "filling the middle space so that the whole is bound together" (202e6–7). For the moment this account leaves unclear the element of "mortality" in Eros, though this absence is soon to be rectified (cf. 203e, 206e7–7a3, 208b5–6): Eros/*erôs* cannot be immortal, because love is love of immortality, which of necessity is something which is lacking to love.

Diotima's threefold division into god, *daimôn*, and man is a systematization and simplification (but one which was to prove very influential) of the much more diffuse and often apparently inconsistent set of ideas about divine beings and forces which characterized Greek society (as many others);[7] it is the kind of classificatory distinction we might have expected from a religious expert, but of itself it is not intended to sound radically innovative (that there are "many *daimones* of all different kinds" [203a6–7] is a view to which most ordinary Greeks would readily have assented). On the other hand, we will not find it difficult to suspect that Socrates himself is the prime example of a "*daimonios* man" who is wise (*sophos*) about *daimones* and the relation between gods and men (203a4–5; for the adjective applied to Socrates, cf. 219c1); Eryximachus, Aristophanes, and Agathon (at least) will, however, not have been pleased to learn that those who are "wise" in the arts are merely "vulgar" (*banausos*).

---

[7] Cf. Burkert (1985) 179–81, 331–32; Osborne (1994) 103–11.

The wonderstruck Socrates now asks a very childlike (cf. 204b1)[8] question about Eros's parents, a notorious problem inviting speculation and invention (cf. 178b2−4). Diotima's answer treats the question at the level it deserves with her simple, childlike fable of Eros's birth from "Poverty" and "Resource, son of Cunning (*Metis*)."[9] Genealogy and personification as devices for explaining the world are familiar to us from Hesiod onward; in the *Republic* Socrates figures philosophy itself as a helpless female who is deserted by those who should support her and left as prey for unworthy men to have their wicked way with her and bring her into disrepute (*Republic* 6.495b8−c6). Not many years before the writing of the *Symposium*, Aristophanes himself had dramatized a confrontation between personified Wealth and Poverty in the *Wealth*. Diotima's simple narrative, which may remind us of Socrates' Aesopic fable of pleasure and pain in the *Phaedo* (cf. above, p. 66), is to be understood as the lowest level of Socrates' instruction; in this, as in everything, Diotima will proceed by orderly stages toward the highest and most difficult mysteries.

The Eros of Diotima's fable inherits his mother's poverty/lack/ want, but from his father he has the "resource" to do something about it (he is again neither one thing nor the other):[10]

> In the first place, he never has any money, and the usual notion that he's sensitive and attractive (*kalos*) is quite wrong: he's a vagrant, with tough, dry skin and no shoes on his feet. He never has a bed to sleep on, but stretches out on the

[8] See Diotima's words to Socrates, "this is obvious even to a child" (204b1); cf., e.g., Socrates' "this is obvious even to a blind man," when *he* is doing the teaching (*Republic* 8.550d6).

[9] If we are to think of Eros as conceived in the normal way, then there is the implication, which is not unimportant for Diotima, that sexual intercourse per se need have nothing to do with *erôs*. Nightingale (1995) 128 n.93 comments, "God knows how Poros managed it while collapsed in a drunken sleep."

[10] For Eros as a resourceful contriver, cf., e.g., Callimachus fr. 67 Pfeiffer (Acontius and Cydippe); Sappho's "guile-weaving daughter of Zeus [i.e., Aphrodite]" (fr. 1.2) is not far away.

ground and sleeps in the open in doorways and by the road-side. He takes after his mother in having need as a constant companion. From his father, however, he gets his ingenuity in going after things of beauty (*kala*) and value (*agatha*), his courage, impetuosity, and energy, his skill at hunting (he's constantly thinking up captivating stratagems), his desire for knowledge, his resourcefulness, his lifelong pursuit of wisdom (*philosophôn*), and his skills with magic, herbs, and words.

He isn't essentially either immortal or mortal. Sometimes within a single day he starts by being full of life in abundance, when things are going his way, but then he dies away . . . only to take after his father and come back to life again. He has an income, but it is constantly trickling away, and consequently Love isn't ever destitute, but isn't ever well off either. He also falls between knowledge and ignorance, and the reason for this is as follows. No god loves knowledge (*philosophei*) or desires wisdom, because gods are already wise; by the same token, no one else who is wise loves knowledge (*philosophei*). On the other hand, ignorant people don't love knowledge or desire wisdom either, because the trouble with ignorance is precisely that if a person lacks virtue and knowledge, he's perfectly satisfied with the way he is. If a person isn't aware of a lack, he can't desire the thing which he isn't aware of lacking. (203c6−4a7)

This mixed being, who bears a striking resemblance to the normally unshod Socrates, ever "scheming after the beautiful and the good" (masculine or neuter?) while exercising a kind of witchcraft upon others (as Alcibiades is soon to confirm; cf. already Agathon at 194a5), "philosophizes throughout life." The philosopher ("lover of wisdom") is not wise, but he restlessly and relentlessly seeks to rid himself of intellectual *aporia* (resourcelessness) and pursues wisdom, which is one of the most beautiful things (204b2−3), possession of which would be true happiness (*eudaimonia*; cf. 204e6−5a3); although the possibility of there being "wise" people is left open (204a2), there is a suggestion here that only gods are truly wise.

Those who are not searching after wisdom, and have no desire to do so, are simply ignorant/stupid (*amatheis*); we cannot fail here to recall Socrates' claim in the *Apology* that, if he is wise, his "wisdom" consists in acknowledging his lack of wisdom (23a–b). That same passage of the *Apology* also offers a splendid illustration of Socrates engaged in the relentless (and to others very annoying) pursuit of understanding.

Diotima moves her argument forward by getting Socrates to agree to the substitution of "good" (*agathon*) for "beautiful" (*kalon*). This potentially problematic substitution is perhaps easier in Greek than in English, given the large semantic overlap of the two Greek words in ordinary usage; moreover, we must never forget that Agathon himself ("Mr. Good") is also the most beautiful (*kallistos*) person at his own party (e.g., 213c5).[11] Nevertheless, these words and ideas are not (for Diotima) simply synonymous or interchangeable; the relationship between them in fact remains somewhat unclear in the *Symposium*, though there will be no doubt that the ultimate object of *erôs*, as of all human activity according to the *Republic* (cf. 6.505a–e), is "[possession of] the good." Be that as it may, this verbal substitution allows Diotima to proceed to consider the ends of action: it is easier for the young Socrates to consider why one wants to possess "good" things rather than "beautiful" things.[12] All human action, the pursuit of "good things and *eudaimonia*," is driven by *erôs*, but whereas language conceals this in the case of, say, money making and even philosophy (we don't say "erotosophy"), it is patent in the case of "lovers" (*erastai*), who are in fact only one instance of a general truth (205d). Having observed that the Aristophanic model as stated must be wrong because it has nothing to say about the "goodness" of the other half which is pursued, Diotima concludes that *erôs* is "of permanent possession of what is good"

[11] Both the meaning of Agathon's name and his beauty are also important in Agathon's other Platonic appearance at *Protagoras* 315d8–e3; cf. also below, p. 98 on Alcibiades' entrance.

[12] Notice how the conversation in 204d–e "mimics" the subject: an answer "desires" a question (*erô-têsis*), and Socrates finds one question easier (*euporô-teron*) than another.

(206a11) and then turns to the central question of what *erôs* does for us.

This second stage of Diotima's exposition, marked as such by Socrates' renewed reference to "seercraft" (206b9), moves away from the Aesopic mode of her earlier fable toward a mystic world of metaphor: *erôs* is "of birth in the beautiful," and it is *erôs* which allows us to bring to birth the "pregnancies" which we carry in our bodies and souls, and this "giving birth" is both something immortal for us and drives us by a desire for immortality, for *erôs* is for immortality as well as for the good.[13] Pregnancy (cf. below, pp. 89–90) here precedes a giving birth, to which the beautiful acts as stimulus and which is described in terms that inevitably suggest (male) ejaculation:

> When what is pregnant draws near to beauty, it becomes obliging and melts with joy, and gives birth and procreates; when, however, it approaches ugliness, it contracts, glum with pain, turns away, curls up, and does not procreate,[14] but retains its unborn children and suffers badly. So the reason why, when pregnant and swollen, ready to burst, it gets so excited in the presence of beauty is that the bearer of beauty releases it from great pain. (206d3–e1)

The metaphorical biology of this and related passages is perhaps (slightly) less strange in Greek than in English, because of an ancient notion (by no means universally held) that male seed contains within itself "embryonic humans" which are placed inside the female womb which then functions merely as a receptacle and hothouse;[15] intercourse and ejaculation may then indeed be seen as a

---

[13] The bibliography on Diotima's mysteries is very large; I am particularly conscious of the influence of Patterson (1991); Ferrari (1992); and Sheffield (2001a), which should be consulted in detail.

[14] The description of the pregnant being turning away from ugliness obviously suggests the detumescence of the penis, and it is hard not to recall Petronius's parody of Virgil, *Satyrica* 132 (of the impotent penis), *illa solo fixos oculos auersa tenebat . . .*

[15] Cf. Aeschylus, *Eumenides* 658–66; Plato, *Timaeus* 91c7–d5; Morrison (1964) 51–55; Pender (1992); Ferrari (2002) 103–4. Halperin (1990) 139–47 is an important commentary on this passage.

kind of "giving birth" (206c5–6).[16] The desire for immortality through procreation is an idea that has exercised a powerful hold over the imagination, and over psychological speculation, for many centuries: in the face of the inevitably transient nature of our bodies, our emotions, and our knowledge, we seek to renew ourselves from within, whether by physical procreation or by the "rehearsal" (*meletê*) of what we knew but are in danger of forgetting (207c9–8b6). The universal desire to overcome the limits of our mortality may be seen also in the *erôs* (208c4–6) of the great figures of myth and history (such as Phaedrus's paradigms of Alcestis and Achilles) to leave a glorious reputation behind them. We all strive to live after death. Despite this universal desire, however, we will suspect that an account which uses "love of honor" (*philotimia*) and "irrational" behavior as evidence (208c2–3) will not (yet) be an adequate or full account of Socrates' own philosophical behavior.

To this point Diotima's account has applied to all human beings, all of whom are pregnant in both body and soul. There are, however, major differences of degree between individuals, so that one can broadly speak of those pregnant in the body and those (more) pregnant in their souls (208e2–9a3). The former seek immortality through children and hence—Diotima speaks from a male perspective— "turn their attention more toward women and are *erôtikoi* in this way." The clear inference is that pregnancy of the soul, which is here privileged over that of the body and to which the remainder of Diotima's discourse will be directed, seeks its outlet in homosexual beauty. Here, then, Pausanias's distinction between the two kinds of *erôs* is recuperated to the service of a challenging thesis. With what are men pregnant in the soul?: "the things which it is fitting for the soul to conceive and give birth to, [namely,] wisdom (*phronêsis*) and the rest of virtue" (209a3–4), particularly moderation and justice. Neither here nor later does Diotima suggest where these "embryos" in the soul might have come from: "intercourse" is entirely devoted to bringing them to birth. In Plato's *Phaedo* and

[16] That intercourse/giving birth is "a divine thing" (206c6) inevitably calls to mind Archilochus fr. 196A West (a seduction scene): "the goddess [Aphrodite] offers many pleasures to young people beyond the divine thing" (vv. 13–15).

Meno knowledge is "recollection" of what our soul has previously learned, but Diotima's entire focus is not on origins, but on the educative process by which such wisdom and virtue is brought to birth; at best, we may perhaps be here encouraged to think of innate potentialities in the soul.

In the *Theaetetus* Socrates presents himself as a midwife who, though barren himself, helps others to bring their ideas to birth and to test their genuineness.[17] In that dialogue also, then, we find a model of "pregnancy," but there Socrates is apparently fashioned as playing a very different role. In the *Symposium* Socrates himself, so we are here to understand, is "pregnant," and it is Socrates who is the prime example of the philosopher en route to that vision of Beauty which makes life worth living (cf. below); as Alcibiades' narrative will make clear, Socrates, who in the *Gorgias* is made to jest that his two *erômenoi* are Alcibiades and philosophy (482a), has long since moved beyond the attractions of individual beauty. Socrates, moreover, is far enough advanced to be able also to act as guide and helper to others (notably Alcibiades), if only they will cooperate, an idea which is at least not completely irreconcilable with the "midwife" model of the *Theaetetus* (cf. below, p. 93). Here Socrates' resemblance to the Eros of Diotima's myth becomes crucial: as Eros is, according to Socrates (now speaking in his own person), the "best coworker" with an individual in the pursuit of truth and immortality (212b4), so Alcibiades, speaking the truth in ignorance, will declare Socrates to be "the best collaborator for becoming as good as possible" (218d3). Alcibiades' understanding of Socrates will, of course, prove limited.

What then is this educative process?:

When someone's mind has been pregnant with virtue from an early age . . . once he reaches the prime of life he longs

[17] Cf. Burnyeat (1977). Attempts to reconcile Diotima's ideas with those of the *Theaetetus* and other dialogues began early; thus a second-century AD commentary on the *Theaetetus* observes that it is "reasonable" that Diotima's "pregnancy of the soul" is the same as the "recollection" idea (*Corpus dei Papiri Filosofici Greci e Latini* III [Florence: 1995] 418–19, col. LVII 15–22).

to procreate and give birth, so he . . . goes around searching for beauty, so that he can give birth there, since he will never do it in ugliness. Since he's pregnant, he prefers physical beauty to ugliness, and he is particularly pleased if he comes across a mind which is attractive (*kalos*), upright, and gifted at the same time. This is a person he immediately finds he can talk fluently to about virtue (lit. has a good resource of *logoi* about virtue) and about what qualities and practices it takes for a man to be good. In short, he takes on this person's education. . . . In other words, once he has come into contact with (lit. touching) beauty and become intimate[18] with it, he produces and gives birth to the offspring he's been pregnant with for so long. (209a8−c3)

Here again Pausanias's prescription is rewritten, but this time to the service of both partners, particularly the "lover." The role of beauty in Plato's thought as productive of creative activity of all kinds—procreation, artistic creation, philosophy—cannot be underestimated; Socrates' habitual association with "beautiful" young men is to be understood both as a stimulus to philosophy, his pursuit of knowledge, and as a metaphor for the unending search for "the beautiful." Whereas Pausanias's *erastês* receives only sexual access from a grateful and "beautiful" partner, here the pregnant lover is offered a beauty (both physical and psychic) in which to give birth (described again in a language suggestive of ejaculation), and what he bears are "words (*logoi*) concerning virtue, the concerns and practices of a good man" (209b8−c1). The partner is certainly offered education of a sort (209c2), and here again we are quite close to Pausanias, but it is the pregnant partner to whom *erôs* is most of service. These *logoi* are "more immortal" than human children, and the couple who was present at their birth (such as Pausanias and Agathon?) share a much stronger "partnership and affection (*philia*)," two words often used in the context of the ideal of marriage, than do a (heterosexual) couple bound together by their children. As proof of this, Diotima

---

[18] The Greek may bear the same double sense as the English.

adduces the "offspring" of Homer, Hesiod, and the other good poets,[19] that is, the poetry which was at the basis of Greek education, and of the great lawgivers such as Lycurgus of Sparta and Solon of Athens; she does not elaborate on what beautiful partners these great names from the past found to facilitate such poetic or legal "births." We ought at this point at least to wonder where Plato's own writings fit into *his* longing for immortality.

To this point Diotima's discourse might be seen as an ingenious elaboration upon more or less familiar metaphors for intellectual activity, such as "giving birth." In Aristophanes' *Frogs*, for example, Dionysus goes down to Hades in search of a "fertile" (*gonimos*) poet (v. 96, a description which puzzles the stolid Heracles), and in the *Clouds* the arrival at the Think Shop of the boorish Strepsiades causes the abortion of a thought. *Erôs* has so far been given a central place by Diotima in the creative and educational process, but it is not one which goes too far beyond areas already sketched out (particularly by Pausanias and Agathon). We still lack an account of the function of *erôs* in Socrates' wisdom, and this would not be the Socrates we know if the climactic position in his (and Diotima's) encomium were to be reserved for the activities of poets and politicians (209a–e), the first two classes whose "wisdom" is popularly celebrated but is found by Socrates in the *Apology* to be worthless, as he seeks to understand the Delphic oracle about himself (*Apology* 21b–22c).

Diotima now makes a fresh start and promises, in the language of the Eleusinian Mysteries, a glimpse of the ultimate and true mystery;[20] "initiation" into *erôs* (cf., e.g., Xenophon, *Symposium* 1.10) was a familiar metaphor, but here it is given quite new life. Metaphor was at the heart of the Mysteries, whose "meaning" was not susceptible to rational demonstration, and so it is to be here also. Just

[19] That a poet's poetry confers a kind of immortality upon him is an idea which becomes very common later; cf. Horace, *Odes* 3.30.6–7; Ovid, *Am.* 1.15.42, *Met.* 15.879, but, for the immortality of poems, we may note already such passages as *Homeric Hymn to Apollo* 172–73; Theognis 237–54; and Thucydides' hope that his history will be a "possession for all time" (1.22.4).

[20] On Diotima's use of the language of the Mysteries, cf. Riedweg (1987) 2–29.

as the conduct of the Mysteries depended on absolute observance of prescribed ritual in due order, so initiation into the final Mysteries of *erôs* similarly requires "correct" (*orthos*) sequencing; it will also prove to be a long process.

The starting point is similar but not identical to Diotima's earlier account: a young man will, through the agency of a guide and *erôs*, fall in love with "a single body" and there generate "beautiful words." He will, however, then come to realize for himself that the beauty in any body is "brother" to the beauty in any other body, so that he might as well consider all bodily beauty one and the same thing and thus become an *erastês* of all beautiful bodies (210a8–b5). The idea that the lover "realizes" this "for himself" is important for understanding the whole of Diotima's account of the philosophical ascent. The account is very thin on details of what the move from one stage to the next actually entails, but the language here strongly suggests that the lover's realization is the result of a "Socratic" process of question-and-answer about whether different manifestations of beauty are or are not in fact manifestations of one and the same quality. In such a "dialectic" exchange, the lover will come to see his own ignorance (as Agathon did) and then be brought to "realize for himself" a higher truth, a realization which will be expressed in *logoi* about the nature of the beauty which attracts him. It is the Socratic/Platonic model of dialectic and cross-examination which best fits Diotima's apparent mixture of "self-advancement" and the important, if somewhat ill defined, role of a "guide" along the way.[21] Here too, then, we find common ground between Diotima's model of philosophical pregnancy and the midwife role which Socrates assigns himself in the *Theaetetus*. It is reasonable to assume that this model of *how* one moves from one stage of the ascent of knowledge to another holds good for every step along the path which Diotima constructs, just as, at every step, it is beauty which is the object of the *logoi*.

[21] The passage at 211c1 has been interpreted as showing that "a guide for the journey is only optional" (Ferrari [1992] 257), but this may put too heavy a weight on "or."

Becoming a lover of "all beautiful bodies" is not mere promiscuity, as our young man will then come to consider that the beauty of souls far surpasses that of bodies; how and on what grounds he will reach this conclusion is again left unstated, though we might again understand that this advance is made through a dialectic consideration of the nature of the beauty which all beautiful bodies manifest. In any case, both the inferiority of bodily beauty to that of the soul and an intimate link between them are familiar Socratic/Platonic ideas. Here, for example, is an exchange between Chaerephon and Socrates about the beautiful and much sought-after *erômenos* Charmides:

> Chaerephon called me and said, "How does the young man strike you, Socrates? Has he not a beautiful face?"
>
> "Very much so," I replied.
>
> "But if he were willing to take his clothes off," he said, "you would think he was faceless, so perfectly beautiful is his body."
>
> The others agreed wholeheartedly with Chaerephon. "Heracles," I exclaimed, "how irresistible you make him out to be, if he also has one other little thing."
>
> "What?" said Critias.
>
> "If the nature of his soul is excellent—and it should be as, Critias, he comes from your house."
>
> "Well," he said, "in that respect too he is truly excellent (*kaloskagathos*)."
>
> "Why then," I said, "do we not undress that part of him and view it rather than his body?" (Plato, *Charmides* 154d1–e6)

The lover in Diotima's account of the Mysteries of *erôs* loves (*erân*) those with good souls and gives birth there to educational *logoi*, "which make young men better" (210c2), a formulation which reuses and gives new meaning to Pausanias's ideal form of pederasty, in which however the focus was on the circumstances under which sexual contact is to be permitted (cf. 184c–85c), a subject in which Socrates has shown no interest. This lack of sexual interest (as narrowly defined) is paradoxically, but powerfully, advertised by the sexual language of the whole of Diotima's discourse, and "making young men better" must also be seen as a provocative reversal of one of the charges on which Socrates was condemned, that of "corrupting young men." (One wonders indeed what Socrates' prosecutor could have done with Diotima's speech.) If we now take stock and ask how this situation differs from that of the production of political and poetic *logoi* in 209b−c, we find that in the former situation, the pregnant male goes around looking for something beautiful in which to give birth, and if he is lucky enough to find someone beautiful in both body and soul, he is immediately more than fertile (209b6−8); there is no sign in this first account either of a guide or of what the pregnant man might have learned along the way. In the second situation, however, which as we have seen strongly suggests a philosophical method associated with both Socrates and Plato, the pregnant man has come to see the importance of recognizing the shared category underlying different particular instances.

Next, the philosophical lover will apply this same ability to recognize family resemblance to the beauty of first, activities and laws, and, then, kinds of knowledge, so that his gaze is fixed on the extraordinary variety of beauty ("the great sea of beauty," 210d4); as he is now in the realm of knowledge he will "give birth to many beautiful and grand *logoi* in boundless philosophy."[22] The next step is almost the final one:

> Anyone who has been guided and trained in the ways of love up to this point, who has viewed things of beauty in the proper order and manner, will now approach the culmination of love's ways and will suddenly catch sight of something of unbelievable beauty—something, Socrates, which in fact gives meaning to all his previous efforts. What he'll see is, in the first place, eternal; it doesn't come to be or cease to be, and it doesn't increase or diminish. In the second place, it isn't beautiful (*kalon*) in one respect and ugly in another, or beautiful at one time but not at another, or beautiful in one setting but ugly in another, or beautiful here and

[22] The implications of this last phrase are particularly contested.

ugly elsewhere, depending on how people find it. Then again, he won't perceive beauty as a face or hands or any other physical feature, or as a piece of reasoning or knowledge, and he won't perceive it as being anywhere else either—in something like a creature or the earth or the heavens. No, he'll perceive it in itself and by itself, constant and eternal, and he'll see that every beautiful object somehow partakes of it, but in such a way that their coming to be and ceasing to be don't increase or diminish it at all, and it remains entirely unaffected.

So the right kind of love for a boy can help you ascend from the things of this world until you begin to catch sight of that beauty, and then you're almost within striking distance of the goal. The proper way to go about or be guided through the ways of love is to start with beautiful things in this world and always make the beauty I've been talking about the reason for your ascent. You should use the things of this world as rungs in a ladder. You start by loving one beautiful body and step up to two; from there you move on to physical beauty in general, from there to the beauty of people's activities, from there to the beauty of intellectual endeavours, and from there you ascend to that final intellectual endeavour, which is no more and no less than the study of that beauty, so that you finally recognise true beauty.

What else could make life worth living . . . than seeing true beauty? If you ever do catch sight of it, gold and clothing and beautiful boys and young men will pale into insignificance beside it. (210e2–11d5)

The ordered training of seeing how an ascending sequence of sets of things shares the same property allows him first to "catch sight of" ("sight" is crucial also in the revelation of the Mysteries) and then to contemplate beauty "itself by itself . . . pure, clean, unmixed" (211b1–2, e1; cf. *Phaedo* 100b6; *Republic* 5.476b10–11, 6.507b), in which all transient beautiful particulars "share in some way" (211b3; cf. *Phaedo* 100c5–6). Here is one of the finest descriptions of Plato's most famous metaphysical concept, the Forms or Ideas, transcendental mental concepts of qualities perfect in their essence, existing beyond time, circumstance, and particular perceptible manifestation. The result of this vision of true Beauty is that the philosophic lover gives birth to true virtue, which is the closest to immortality a man can attain. Diotima's ideas and language about what philosophy is are here (unsurprisingly) close to those of Socrates in the *Republic*:

> A genuine lover of knowledge innately aspires to reality, and doesn't settle on all the various things which are assumed to be real, but keeps on, with his love remaining keen and steady, until the nature of each thing as it really is in itself has been grasped by the appropriate part of his mind—which is to say, the part which is akin to reality. Once he has drawn near this authentic reality and united with it, and thus fathered intellect and truth, then he has knowledge; then he lives a life which is true to himself; then he is nourished; and then, not before, he finds release from his love-pangs. (Plato, *Republic* 6.490a8–b7; trans. Waterfield)

Diotima's account is something of which Socrates is firmly persuaded (212b2); the choice of language acknowledges the account's special status as a revelation of that which may be beyond formal proof (cf. *Republic* 10.621c1, after the myth of Er, "the myth could save us, if we are persuaded by it").[23] Certainly, it may be beyond Socrates' fellow guests, whose praise for the speech (212c4) is not glossed in any way that suggests understanding or a wish to engage with it; only Aristophanes is moved to intervene because he recognizes an allusion to his own speech. Socrates has shown us what *erôs*, properly understood, actually is, what function beauty has in leading us up the ladder of knowledge, and what *erôs* can do for us in terms of virtue and understanding; throughout his speech, and that

[23] Cf. also *Gorgias* 524a8–b1, 526d3–4; *Phaedo* 108e, 109a7.

of Diotima, we recognize fragments of the ideas of earlier speeches put to the service of a new encomiastic vision. It is a vision which has, of course, a very different effect from that of the other speeches. Its apparent rejection of the value of lasting love between individuals has often seemed to modern readers to present a harshly intellectual view of *erôs* which ignores basic, universal facts of human experience and which offers little comfort to all but a Socrates.[24] Like the hero of an epic or a tragedy, however, the Socrates of the *Symposium* embodies ideals to which we may aspire, but—though this is something which neither Aristodemus nor Apollodorus understood—he is not set before us as a model to be copied (even if we could). Alcibiades' speech will suggest both why Socratic *erôs* may be beyond most of us and how we should use the "idea" of Socrates in more productive ways.

2 | Alcibiades

Alcibiades' first words, heard from the court outside, work like a pun on the speeches of Socrates and Diotima: "he was very drunk and shouting loudly, asking where Agathon was and demanding that someone lead him to Agathon" (212d3−5).[25] Diotima has just explained the way in which each of us may be led toward the truly good (*agathon*) and beautiful, but it was not a flute-girl and slaves (212d6−7) she had in mind for that role; the serious (*spoudaion*) and the metaphysical have given way to the humorous (*geloion*) and the all too physical with brilliant suddenness. The juxtaposition of Diotima's "mysteries" and Alcibiades' riotous entrance inevitably evokes the charge against him of having profaned the Eleusinian Mysteries (above, p. 14); on this occasion, however, we will be given an immediate chance to hear his speech of defense.

[24] Cf., e.g., Vlastos (1973) chapter 1; Nussbaum (1986) chapter 6.
[25] On ideas of "leading" and "guiding" throughout the *Symposium*, cf. Osborne (1994) chapter 4.

Alcibiades' speech will pick up Diotima's, for he will deliver an encomium upon Socrates (the object of his own paradoxical *erôs*) rather than upon Eros, but Diotima's speech has shown us how very alike these two "creatures" in fact are.[26] The "mysteries" of Love which he will reveal will also show him embracing (indeed with his arms around) "truth" (219b7), but again not quite as Diotima envisaged (212a4−5). The end of Alcibiades' great speech similarly picks up the end of Diotima's speech. Whereas she had spoken of the way in which true virtue may be brought to birth (in the shape of *logoi*) through coming to see the truth (212a3−7), Alcibiades acknowledges that Socrates' words carry "images of virtue" within them (222a4).[27] Alcibiades' performance for the invited guests is thematized by Plato as a playful and rather naughty satyr drama;[28] tragedians entered three tragedies and a final satyr play in the great Dionysiac contests, and the satyr play often reflects upon the tragedies which have preceded from an oblique, and very Dionysiac, angle. Alcibiades, stories of whose "satyric" fondness for wine and komastic adventure fill the anecdotal tradition,[29] the very antithesis— one might have thought—of a female seer who can control and even laugh at Socrates, turns the sober world of Agathon's symposium upside down: now it is *erômenoi*, not their lovers, who get insanely jealous (213c−d); it is they who are enslaved to their teachers (215e6−7, 216b5−6, 219e4, and so on); and it is sexual abstinence which is characterized as outrage (*hybris*, 219c5). Alcibiades will, however, align himself with Socrates in telling only "the truth" (214a6−15a2).

[26] The detailed parallels between the two speeches have been noted by many; cf., e.g., Bury (1932) lx−lxii; Riedweg (1987) 14−16; Sheffield (2001b) 196−97.

[27] The parallelism is pointed by the similarity between 212b1 ("This, Phaedrus and you others, is what Diotima said . . . ") and 222a7 ("This, gentlemen, is my encomium of Socrates . . . ").

[28] Cf. below, pp. 100−101; Sheffield (2001b); Usher (2002). For a full bibliography and discussion of the themes of satyr drama, cf. Griffith (2002).

[29] The standard discussion of literary representations of Alcibiades is Gribble (1999); see also Wohl (1999). The speaker of Lysias 14 turns Alcibiades' son into a good replica of his "debauched" father (note esp. 14.24).

Alcibiades likens[30] the snub-nosed, pot-bellied Socrates and the way he talks to the crafted image of a conventionally ugly Silenus or satyr, carrying musical pipes (*auloi*). When the statue is opened up, it reveals smaller images of the gods inside (215a6–b3); the warning against "assuming homology between visible appearance and the reality within,"[31] a mistake against which much of Platonic philosophy is directed, seems clear. Literature and iconography both reveal the continuing power of this image of Socrates as a Silenus (cf. Xenophon, *Symposium* 4.19, 5.7), an image which may have started as abusive mockery but was soon recuperated (perhaps by Socrates himself).[32] Alcibiades draws upon stories about the chief of all such figures, old Father Silenus himself, a source of ancient and secret wisdom; this Dionysiac creature, like Diotima's Eros neither god nor man nor beast, taught Dionysus himself, as Socrates "taught" Alcibiades, the living Dionysus. It is, however, also important that the image of Socrates as a Silenus is Alcibiades'; it is not one which, at least as Alcibiades uses it, we must assume comes with special (Platonic) authority. It is perhaps less important that the image would contradict Socrates' repeated assertion of his own lack of knowledge than that it presents a completed, unchanging figure who already has "all he needs" (particularly all the knowledge), whereas both Diotima and Socrates himself have led us to believe that the philosopher is engaged in a constant search to remedy his lack.

If the Silenus image seems to reuse Diotima's images of pregnancy at a lower, more comic level, and Alcibiades offers his body as a place into which Socrates might "give birth" (though that is not, presumably, how Alcibiades would have described it), Alcibiades is in fact, like Diotima's Poverty, seeking to remedy his own lack by acquiring Socrates' images, and that is precisely not how

[30] For this sympotic game, cf. above, p. 5. The bibliography on Alcibiades' *eikōn* is very large; I have found particular help in Steiner (1996); for the implications of the *aulos*, cf. Wilson (1999) 88–91. Further discussion and bibliography are in Blondell (2002) 70–72.

[31] Steiner (2001) 89.

[32] Cf. Zanker (1995) 32–39.

Socratic *erôs* works. The depth of Alcibiades' misunderstanding is thus revealed when he explains that he assumed that, in return for sexual favors, he would "hear everything which Socrates knew" (217a4–5). This is not the model of Socratic inquiry with which we are familiar; Socrates' "failure" to enlighten Alcibiades as to his misconceptions is as powerful a reminder of that as we could wish. Alcibiades, who claims to know what lies behind Socrates' appearance, has once more been misled by appearances: Socrates is indeed a paradoxical satyr, who does *seem* not to need anything such as food, drink, money, warm clothing, or sex. He appears entirely self-sufficient; even his thirst for conversation with pretty young men (216d2–4) is just a game. The absolute opposite of the mass of contradictions which is Alcibiades himself, Socrates appears as unchanging as Diotima's ultimate Beauty (210e6–b5), never having great enthusiasms and desires, never out of control, lacking nothing (least of all, public admiration).

Socrates is, moreover, not just any Silenus, but a Marsyas, the satyr who fatally challenged Apollo in musical skill and whose music is used in ritual initiations for its qualities of manic possession; a pity, then, that Alcibiades does not realize how Socrates could in fact initiate him (cf. 210a1). Listening to Socrates induces a manic state, not unlike the symptoms of love ("heart leaps, tears pour forth," 215e1–2), such as no other speaker can weave. Socrates' philosophical *logoi* should not, of course, produce an emotional response more associated with tragedy or rhetoric (at least as a Gorgias saw the power of such verbal performances),[33] but Alcibiades' description is a typically extravagant version of a familiar aspect of Plato's picture of Socrates; very close to Alcibiades' portrait is that of Meno, who is also forced to fall back on "likenesses":

> Socrates, before I as much as made your acquaintance I had heard that you are simply perplexed yourself (lit. in *aporia*) and that you make others perplexed as well; and now, as it

[33] Cf. above, p. 74. Bacon (1959) 425 sees the likeness as a productive one: "it is pity and fear not for an actor on the stage, but for himself, when . . . forced . . . to confront himself, and recognize that his life is no better than a slave's."

seems to me, you are bewitching me with magic and altogether putting a spell on me,[34] so that I am completely at a
loss (lit. full of *aporia*). And you seem to me, if I may actually make a joke, to be altogether most like, both in appearance and in other respects, to that flat sea-fish, the electric
ray. For this causes whoever at any time comes close to it and
comes into contact with it to be numb; and I think you too
have now done something like this to me. For I am truly
numbed both in my mind and in my speech, and I have no
answer to give you. And yet I have on countless occasions
said a great deal about excellence to many people, and very
well too, at least as I thought; but now I can't even say at all
what it is. I think you make a right decision in not traveling
abroad from here or living abroad; for if you did such things
as a foreigner in another city, you might well be arrested as
a wizard. (Plato, *Meno* 79e7–80b7; trans. R. W. Sharples)

The Socratic spell has, however, not just reduced Alcibiades to
philosophical *aporia*, but to thinking that, in his present condition,
life is not worth living (216a1), although we, at least, know from
Diotima that Socrates can in fact help one toward a glimpse of the
only thing which does indeed make life worth living (211d2–3).
Alcibiades does know (at some level) that it is Socrates alone who
can offer the answer, but political ambition and the love of honor
keep driving him elsewhere, his ears blocked like Odysseus's witless
crew confronted with the Sirens (216a7);[35] these Homeric creatures
lured men, who thirsted after knowledge, through the fact that they
claimed to know "all that happened on the earth" (*Odyssey* 12.189–
91). Alcibiades makes a deliberate choice to avoid hearing the Song
of Socrates, because such an education would get in the way of political success (216a5–8); at another level, however, he knows that it
is with Socrates that he should be. Such self-knowledge, the real-

[34] The language here is very close to Diotima's description of *erôs* at 203d8.

[35] For a generalization of this type of behavior see *Republic* 6.494c–5b. We may
also be reminded of midwife Socrates' regret for those who have left him too early
and thus "miscarried through keeping bad company" (*Theaetetus* 150e4–5).

ization that he is harming himself by yielding to baser desires and drives, has led to a kind of self-loathing.

There is a clear apologetic aspect to these words which Plato has placed in Alcibiades' mouth. Despite what rumor and his accusers said, Socrates had no control or influence over the turbulent political career of his most high-profile young associate; Socrates and politics tugged in very different directions. Outside Plato, Alcibiades was a prominent subject in much Socratic literature, and this reflects the special problem which his relationship with Socrates posed for those who sought to fashion Socrates' posthumous reputation; Polycrates' lost *Accusation of Socrates* certainly exploited the potential of this relationship to arouse prejudice against Socrates. The surprise (and risk) of the brilliant literary masterstroke by which Plato makes Alcibiades himself deliver an encomium of Socrates is thus not to be underrated.

Xenophon too devotes a lengthy section at the beginning of the *Memorabilia* to seeking to dispel prejudice which Socrates may have incurred from his association with Alcibiades. According to Xenophon, Alcibiades, together with Socrates' relation Critias, was the "most politically ambitious" of all the Athenians (1.2.14) and thought that Socrates could teach him "to speak and act"; while with Socrates he prospered and did no harm, but his ambition took him away, where he was ruined by the attentions of women and lesser men and so "neglected himself" (1.2.24; cf. *Symp.* 216a5–6). Far from incurring blame, therefore, Socrates is, in Xenophon's view, to be praised for the controlling influence he exercised on Alcibiades while he was young. In his erotic dialogue, the *Amatorius*, in which allusions to the *Symposium* abound, Plutarch too spells out one inference which may be drawn from the speech of the Platonic Alcibiades by having a character tell how a drunk Alcibiades burst in ("on a *kômos*") to the house of Anytus, famous later as Socrates' chief prosecutor, and stole some of his expensive cups; in this anecdote also, Alcibiades is clearly the *erômenos* and his behavior is explicitly characterized as "hubristic" by an observer.[36] What is most

[36] Plutarch, *Amatorius* 762c; cf. *Life of Alcibiades* 4.5.

important, however, in Plutarch's narrative is Alcibiades' relations with the man responsible for Socrates' death; Alcibiades' promiscuity of association is, so we are to understand, the clearest possible indication of Socrates' lack of responsibility for the actions which damaged Athens.

If Xenophon has similar apologetic purposes to those of Plato, there is also a revealing difference. Xenophon presents Socrates as a teacher, like a teacher of musical instruments (*Memorabilia* 1.2.27), whose discipline ends when the pupil leaves him. Plato's Socrates, on the other hand, is not, as Diotima's speech and the whole Platonic corpus makes clear, a "teacher" in that way. Xenophon deals with Socrates' accusers on their own terms, whereas Plato constructs his own Socrates and his own Socratic myth. The distraction which Socrates induces ("I have no idea what to do with this man"), made manifest in a desire to be rid of him which competes with the knowledge of how terrible such a loss would be (216b6–c3), suggests (with painful irony) the attitude of the Athenians as a whole both to Socrates and indeed to Alcibiades himself (cf. Aristophanes, *Frogs* 1425: "the city longs for him, it hates him, it wants to have him"); more potently, perhaps, it suggests a condition which many would recognize as love.[37]

Whereas Diotima's instruction had proceeded through question-and-answer, through myth, and through revelation, Alcibiades moves from "images" to the confirming autobiographical mode of legal speeches; Agathon's guests are to pass judgment upon his story, or rather upon Socrates' "contemptuous superiority" (219c5–6). It is here hard not to think of another trial, in which Socrates was accused of "corrupting young men" and in which his habitually "strange" behavior counted heavily against him; in the *Apology* (19c2–5) Plato makes Socrates refer to his first entrance in the *Clouds*, hanging in a basket and proclaiming "to tread the air and get his mind around the sun," a claim which Strepsiades understands as confirming that Socrates "puts his mind above that of the gods" (*Clouds* 225–26).

[37] Thus Catullus 85 (*odi et amo* . . .) is very close to the Aristophanic verse. The most thought-provoking account of Alcibiades' love for Socrates is probably Nussbaum (1986) chapter 6.

In what such "superiority" consists, we are presently to learn. Would *we* condemn such a man?

Alcibiades replaces the *erastês* and *erômenos* of Pausanias's ideal model by autobiographical history: he explains how he realized the worth of what Socrates had apparently to offer, and assumed that what Socrates would want in return was sexual access to his young body. He therefore arranged various opportunities (including naked wrestling) for Socrates to make sexual approaches, but nothing of the kind happened,[38] to Alcibiades' considerable puzzlement (he would presumably have been surprised to learn that, based on Diotima's account, Socrates was actually "giving birth" inside him during their conversations). Alcibiades here, of course, is by his own admission acting more like a frustrated *erastês* than an *erômenos*, or (and this comparison is even less flattering) like an *erômenos* who shamefully sells himself; when Socrates later charges him with trying to "exchange gold for bronze" (219a1), we should be conscious of the monetary resonance. Socrates' apparent disinterest in Alcibiades' body, a phenomenon which Diotima's speech has allowed us (but not Alcibiades) to understand, is itself a provocation to inquiry (217c6: "I had to know what was going on").

Alcibiades' version of the most secret mystery is, as is proper, spoken only to those who have been initiated into the "philosophic madness and Bacchic frenzy" (218b3–4),[39] a phrase not only appropriate to the sympotic setting, but also one which takes us back to the comparison of Socrates to Marsyas with his maddening piping.[40] This is also one of a number of "we're all alone" passages which play with the idea of a large audience of eavesdroppers upon a symposium, or rather with readers of the *Symposium* (all of whom,

---

[38] In the *Republic* Socrates assumes that exercising together and persistent proximity will lead "through the compulsions of nature" to sex between male and female guardians (*Republic* 5.458d2–3), but Socrates is made of even sterner stuff.

[39] For other aspects of this passage, cf. above, p. 14. How Platonic this idea is may be gauged by the contrast with Xenophon, *Symposium* 1.4, where Callias tells Socrates and his companions that he would like them as guests because they are "purified in their souls."

[40] Cf., e.g., *Laws* 7.815c for these associations.

to some extent, will have been touched by the "philosophic madness"). The mystery which Alcibiades relates is the narrative of the occasion on which he saw the images inside Socrates and they appeared to him "divine and golden and all beautiful and amazing" (216e7–17a1), an idiosyncratic version, of course, of the philosopher's vision of the amazing, unchanging, divine Beauty with which Diotima's speech concluded. "Philosophic madness" cannot fail to suggest to us Socrates' mystical account in the *Phaedrus* of precisely the "madness" of the philosopher whose soul ascends to the realm of the Forms (245b–50c6), an account which shares important features with Diotima's final mystery; clearly, no one at Agathon's party except Socrates qualifies as an initiate into philosophic madness under the account of the *Phaedrus*, but Alcibiades is here rather drunkenly repeating and reworking his earlier comparison of the effect of Socratic arguments to the music which rouses and possesses members of ecstatic cults (215c–e). It is obvious from whom Alcibiades has heard the "*logoi* in philosophy" (218a5).

In order to understand how Alcibiades got his wires crossed, it is necessary to go back again to Pausanias's ideal situation:

> If in any meeting between a lover and his boyfriend each has his set of guidelines—the lover appreciating that any service he performs for a boyfriend who gratifies him would be morally acceptable, and the boy appreciating that any favours he does for a man who is teaching him things and making him good would be morally acceptable, the lover capable of increasing wisdom and other aspects of goodness, the boy eager to learn and generally to increase his knowledge—it is only then, when these facets of the moral code coincide, that it becomes all right for a boy to gratify a lover. Under any other circumstances, it is wrong. (184d3–e4)

> On the same principle, suppose someone is led by a lover's putative goodness to gratify him in the expectation of gaining, for his part, moral benefit from the lover's friendship, but his hopes are dashed: the man turns out to be a scoundrel and to have no goodness to his name. Even so, being de-

ceived in this way is all right, because the aspect of himself which he is seen to have shown is that he'd gladly do anything and everything for the sake of moral improvement, and there's nothing more creditable than that. So there's absolutely nothing wrong with gratifying a lover for the sake of virtue. (185a5–b5)

Alcibiades does indeed believe that Socrates can make him "wise and good," can make him "a better person"; he offers Socrates his body because it would be "senseless" (218c9) not to do so (on Pausanias's model). One of the things which Alcibiades has not recognized, however, is that his many conversations with Socrates (217b6–7) were not only part of Socrates' restless search, part of his "giving birth in the beautiful," but were precisely guiding Alcibiades on a journey which could have resulted in him becoming "better." Socrates' *erôs*, as Diotima has allowed us to glimpse, is not for any individual beautiful body, and not indeed for bodies at all. His words to Alcibiades contain for us echoes of Diotima's revelation, to make the point that—from another perspective—Socrates could indeed help Alcibiades along the way:

> It would be an irresistible beauty (*amêchanon kallos*) that you would see in me. . . . you are trying to acquire truly beautiful things (lit. the truth of beautiful things) in exchange for the apparently beautiful (lit. the appearance [of beautiful things]). (218e2–6)

From Alcibiades' point of view, there is nothing in Socrates' speech to suggest that the latter will now refuse the opportunity for sex; rather, it is perfectly possible to read the speech as an acceptance of Alcibiades' offer, but one expressed in the typically "ironic" (218d6) and self-deprecatory Socratic manner. It is Alcibiades' very familiarity with that manner, with, for example, the typically Socratic contrast between "truth" and "appearance" (218e6), which leads to his misunderstanding of Socrates' words; the same is true of Socrates' reply at 219a8–b2, in which he corrects Alcibiades' singular imperative ("you yourself give thought to what is best for us") to an invitation to a Socratic joint investigation ("in the time to come we will take thought").[41] If it is only subsequent reflection and further experience of Socrates which has brought Alcibiades to the ironic interpretation of Socrates' words, that increased understanding has colored his narrative of recollection.

The night which Alcibiades spends with Socrates continues the catalog of his misunderstanding. Though he has pursued Socrates like an *erastês*, when lying down with him he waits passively[42] like an *erômenos* for the older man to become sexually aroused and seek physical relief. Alcibiades only has himself to blame if Socrates too now plays to perfection the (passive) *erômenos* role in which he has been cast by Alcibiades himself. Plato has created a hilarious comedy about who is supposed to do what to whom. From another perspective, Socrates' apparent imperviousness to physical desire can also be understood as one more remarkable *epideixis* by the philosopher. It is interpreted by Alcibiades (who himself knew all about *hybris*) as scornful ridicule of his beauty, just as the soldiers on campaign think that Socrates' apparent imperviousness to the cold is a way of mocking them (220b7−8); with Socrates, however, appearances are almost always deceptive. From one perspective, Alcibiades is near a kind of truth: a major step in the philosopher's progress—and we at least will now read Socrates in the light of Diotima's "program"—is indeed to "scorn and think little of" (210b5−6) the single beautiful body to which he was first attached, though there is nothing to suggest that Alcibiades played this role in Socrates' life. Nevertheless, such remarkable feats of endurance and control (*thaumasia*, 221c2) are the stuff of which myth is made, and Alcibiades' encomiastic strategy is indeed to shape Socrates into a figure

---

[41] The exchange irresistibly calls to mind (once again) the seduction scene of Archilochus's "Cologne epode" (fr. 196A West): "I and you will take thought for this with the god's help. . . ." Nehamas (1998) 59−61 offers a helpful discussion of Alcibiades' "misunderstanding" of Socrates.

[42] For the unaroused passivity (at least in the ideology of pederasty) of the *erômenos*, cf. Dover (1978) 94−97; a famously stern view is that of the Xenophontic Socrates at *Symp.* 8.21: "Unlike a woman, a boy does not share in the delights of love-making, but sober looks on at the other drunk with desire."

around whom anecdote and myth cluster (like Ajax, 219e2). Socrates' calm normality during the retreat at Delium (221a–b) is precisely the stuff of legend.

Of particular interest is Alcibiades' comparison—for the latter part of his speech reverts to the use of likenesses—of Socrates to Odysseus, through quotation of a verse used by both Helen and Menelaus in the fourth book of the *Odyssey* in their accounts of Odysseus's exploits of bravery and self-control at Troy (220c2). The second of these passages (Menelaus's) establishes Odysseus as, like Socrates, a "one-off":

> Before now I have come to know the counsel and the mind of many heroic men, and I have travelled far over the earth, but I have never seen with my eyes such a man as was Odysseus of the much-enduring heart. What a thing was this too which that strong man did in the carved horse, where all we Argive chiefs were sitting to bring death and slaughter to the Trojans. (Homer, *Odyssey* 4.267–73)

In the wooden horse Odysseus had resisted Helen's deceptive use of the voices of the Greeks' wives and had, single-handedly, prevented others from doing so also; in this way "he saved all the Achaeans" (*Od.* 4.288). We have already seen Socrates' immunity to sexual temptation, and Alcibiades will proceed to give examples of how Socrates performed heroic services of communal benefit in wartime, though conventional civic motives such as "honor" seem very far away; here is a living embodiment of the bravery (*andreia*) of *erôs* of which Phaedrus and Agathon have spoken.[43] Socrates' solitary self-absorption is perhaps being compared to Odysseus's patient, silent plotting against the suitors on his return home, but Odysseus, the hero "of many turns," was to have a very long afterlife as the model for the restless inner search, the quest for knowledge of the philosopher, and indeed as a heroic model for Socrates.

[43] For a wry look at Socrates' heroism, cf. Brecht's short story "Der verwundete Sokrates" (*Gesammelte Werke* [Frankfurt: 1967] V 286–303).

Alcibiades will, however, make the point that the most extraordinary thing about Socrates is that, though one might compare him in particular respects to, say, Odysseus, "he is like no other man, either of the ancients nor those of the present day" (221c4–5); Socrates has, in his totality, no model or equal to whom he may be likened, as the great Spartan general Brasidas may be likened to Achilles or the great Athenian statesman Pericles to Nestor. Socrates in fact, appealing with rhetorical skill and interpretive inventiveness to the epic poetry beloved of the jurors, had claimed Achilles as a model for himself in the *Apology* (28c1–d4): both he and Achilles placed concerns of *dikê* (justice, revenge) above fear of death. This is exactly the same Achillean motif which Phaedrus had put to a different use in his speech (179e1–80b5), but the example of Brasidas suggests that Alcibiades at least is not thinking of Achilles' devotion to either justice or Patroclus, but rather of his military prowess. The choice of one Spartan (Brasidas) and one Athenian (Pericles) is a wry hint at Alcibiades' checkered political history, for he served both of these states, equally well and equally badly, in their destructive war with each other (cf. above, p. 4); nevertheless, there is also a particular point in Alcibiades' stress upon the "incomparability" of Socrates. Alcibiades himself incurred hatred in Athens because of his "out-of-the-ordinariness" (*paranomia*).[44] Democracy entails a leveling of the citizens, and those whose "strangeness" (*atopia*) cannot be leveled out, who cannot be "likened" to known categories, are likely to pay the penalty; the state no more knew what to do with either Alcibiades or Socrates than Alcibiades knew what to do with Socrates. In both their cases, it was Athens which was the loser (cf. Thucydides 6.15.4).

Epic poetry and its descendant, tragedy, Agathon's genre, tell the stories of the great men of the past, and the meaning of those stories resides not in their literal historicity, whether they happened or not, but in the patterns of behavior which are instantiated in them. Poetry is a special case of the familiar truth that people tell

---

[44] Cf. Gribble (1999) 69–82; the hostile speaker of [Andocides] 4.24 notes that the like of Alcibiades had never been seen before.

tales about the past (inter alia) to try to explain the present to themselves. Alcibiades is telling "true" stories about one of his contemporaries, but for Plato's audience, as for us, Socrates was a great figure from the past to whom many stories attached:

> [Plato] treats historical characters with the fluidity of myth. He recreates the Athens of his childhood as a "legendary" past in which he locates "real" people for the exploration of his own concerns. As such it is populated with the heroes and villains of his imagination, and provides an ancestry and aetiology for the problems and concerns, political and ideological, of his own time.[45]

No doubt, by the middle of the fourth century, Socrates, like Alcibiades himself, was the subject of considerable anecdotal material, but there is one particular kind of memory of Socrates which is crucial here, and that of course is the Socratic dialogue, most notably Plato's Socratic dialogues. They are a literary form with their own hero,[46] and if we are too concerned with narrow questions of historicity, whether of setting or of characters or of the views which are ascribed in the dialogues to Socrates, we will be missing the point. Thus, as the sequence of encomia draws to a close, we return to the issues which were central to the opening frame, namely, the Socratic legend (how ought we to remember him?), the growth of writing about Socrates, and how to read a Socratic dialogue. Socrates was of course much more than just "good to think with," but he was indeed a vehicle through which Plato explored his own vision. As such, both we and Plato must acknowledge that the Socratic dialogue is like, as well as very unlike, the great poetry which claimed to educate the Athenians.

We return in another way also to the issues of the frame. The source for Apollodorus's story is Aristodemus who, as we have already noted, copied the externals of Socratic behavior (shoelessness and so on), though there is no sign that he got very far on the

---

[45] Blondell (2002) 33.
[46] Cf. Clay (2000) 51–59; Hobbs (2000).

philosophic journey. Despite Aristodemus, imitation of Socrates is a charge, or perhaps a badge of pride, which many philosophers from the fourth century on, of varying intellectual gifts, thoroughly deserve. How can *we* imitate Socrates, and should we try? Alcibiades notes that one can look at the poetry of the past and find there "equivalents" for the great figures of the modern world. It is a small step from there to the idea of educational mimesis, of treating those figures as models after whom we should fashion our lives, or at least recognizing (as Plato certainly did) how hearing and watching those characters does influence us. No doubt Plato would have wanted the *Symposium* to influence its readers, but he has gone out of his way to cancel the possibility of any simple mimesis of the great figure at its center: we can no more imitate Socrates' satyric appearance or his inner virtue than we can "do philosophy" simply by reading the *Symposium*. At best, perhaps, we will learn from Alcibiades' experience (222b5–7) and realize that it is with ourselves, not with our teachers, that we must begin.

·4·

The Morning After

1 | The Imagined Past

The *Symposium* has always been one of Plato's most read, most influential, and most imitated works. No doubt this has much to do with the universal appeal of its subject matter—no Greek text is, for example, cited more often in Roland Barthes's famous *Lover's Discourse*[1]—but it is also the rich variety of the work, together with its accessibility to readers with little philosophical training, which have given it a place of honor in the reception of Platonic ideas. Unsurprisingly, of course, some parts—Pausanias's "Two Venuses," the speeches of Aristophanes (cited as early as Aristotle) and Diotima, the entry of Alcibiades (depicted by, inter alios, Rubens, Testa, and Feuerbach),[2] Alcibiades' night with Socrates—have proved more memorable and worthy of allusion than others, but the work as a whole has shaped the way that the "golden age" of classical Athens has been imagined.

[1] Barthes (1978).

[2] Cf. McGrath (1983); Henderson (forthcoming). Feuerbach's three versions are figures 78–80 in G. Keyssner (ed.), *Feuerbach: Eine Auswahl aus dem Lebenswerk des Meisters in 108 Abbildungen* (Stuttgart/Berlin: 1921).

Plato almost seems to have designed the *Symposium* for those who like their history presented in clear synoptic snapshots: in one room we have gathered glittering representatives of art, science, philosophy, and politics, that heady mixture of intellectual and imperial power that is precisely the modern vision of Athens in the later decades of the fifth century. Moreover, this is a "prelapsarian" Athens, situated just before the disasters of the last years of the century, after which, in the standard model of popular history, there was to be no return to the golden age. That those disasters are clearly foreshadowed within the work merely adds to our (manipulable) sense of regret for an irrecoverable and better past; we may perhaps compare it to all those modern books and films which depict English society before the First World War as a place of glorious innocence about to be shattered forever. A parallel rather closer to Plato would be the modern popular sense of the Funeral Speech, which Thucydides places in the mouth of Pericles in the second book of his *Histories*: this too is viewed, and may in part have been viewed by Thucydides himself, as a glorious (last) testament to a remarkable society which was soon to be brought low by military failure, overweening personal ambition (of which Alcibiades stands as the prime example), and the petty squabbling of "smaller" men. If Thucydides' Pericles speaks to us directly, the characters of the *Symposium* are recreated for us through a veil of hearsay and secondhand reports, which seems to dramatize both our own frantic efforts to discover "what actually happened" in the Athenian past and the impossibility of ever being sure. There is so much we have to take on trust; to cover up our ignorance and the insecurity which goes with it, we are forever, just like Apollodorus and Plato, putting words into the mouths of "historical" characters, making them say what we would like them to have said. The *Symposium* feeds both our sense of insecurity about the past and our indomitable hopefulness that, despite everything, we are in touch with it.

The subject of the *Symposium*, erotic desire, is central to the historical nostalgia which the work has at various times generated. Despite Pausanias's rhetorical and ethical contortions, despite the hierarchies of types of desire to which almost all the speakers adhere, and despite the complexities in Greek attitudes toward sexual relations which much recent scholarship has so fully explored, the *Symposium* has often been represented as a witness to an age which both recognized and openly celebrated the place of *erôs* in human lives and the many forms that such desire may take. For those who wish to see Greek sexuality as less ridden with guilt, less saddled with hang-ups than almost any society of modern times—often, of course, in order to urge their own societies to adopt more liberal, more "Greek" attitudes—there will always be something to be found in the *Symposium*. Allusions to this work run, for example, as something of a leitmotif through E. M. Forster's novel *Maurice*, first written in 1913–1914 but only published posthumously in 1971. The novel tells the story of Maurice Hall and Clive Durham coming to terms with their homosexual feelings and their "Platonic" love for each other while undergraduates at Cambridge; whereas Clive loses his love and his love affair with an imaginary Greece, becomes "normal," and marries a woman, Maurice finally finds emotional and physical satisfaction with a young male gamekeeper. It is the older, more scholarly Clive, whose eyes had first been opened by the *Phaedrus*,[3] who introduces Maurice to Plato's work:

> Towards the end of term they touched upon a yet more delicate subject. They attended the Dean's translation class, and when one of the men was forging quietly ahead Mr Cornwallis observed in a flat toneless voice: "Omit: a reference to the unspeakable vice of the Greeks." Durham observed afterwards that he ought to lose his fellowship for such hypocrisy.
>
> Maurice laughed,
> "I regard it as a point of pure scholarship. The Greeks, or most of them, were that way inclined, and to omit it is to omit the mainstay of Athenian society."
> "Is that so?"
> "You've read the *Symposium*?"

[3] Pp. 61–62. All subsequent references in the text are to Forster (1971).

Maurice had not, and did not add that he had explored Martial.

"It's all in there—not meat for babes, of course, but you ought to read it. Read it this vac." (pp. 42–43)

Clive subsequently prefaces his first declaration of love to Maurice with another reference to the *Symposium*— "I knew you read the *Symposium* in the vac. . . . Then you understand—without me saying more " (p. 50; cf. pp. 55, 81)—and certain scenes in the book may be read as versions of motifs from the *Symposium*: Maurice trying to get Clive alone like Alcibiades' maneuverings around Socrates (pp. 54–56), and Clive's enthusiastic lecture to Maurice on aesthetics as a "giving birth to *logoi* in the beautiful" (pp. 82–83). For Forster, as for many intellectuals of the time, Plato offered almost the only available language in which homosexual feelings could seriously be discussed.[4]

In a "terminal note" to *Maurice*, written in 1960, Forster says that the novel was inspired by a visit to his friend Edward Carpenter, the socialist educator and writer who believed "in the Love of Comrades, whom he sometimes called Uranians" (p. 235). This last term, derived from the high-minded *erôs* depicted by Plato's Pausanias (from whom the term "Pausanian" was also created for a similar "ideal"), was applied to themselves by various aesthetes and poets in the last decades of the nineteenth century and the early ones of the twentieth. The Uranians pursued, as they saw it, a higher ideal of pure homosexual (and often pederastic) love descending from Plato.[5] Carpenter himself published an anthology of passages relating to "friendship" (*Iolaus: Anthology of Friendship*) in which the *Symposium* and the *Phaedrus* bulk large. In *Maurice*, the unconsummated, and ultimately doomed, passion of Maurice and Clive, which Forster described as "precarious, idealistic and peculiarly English"

[4] Helpful discussion is in Jenkyns (1980) 280–93.

[5] Cf. Smith (1970). For Carpenter's reflections on this subject, cf. Carpenter (1923) 130–68; for "Pausanian" cf., e.g., A. L. Raile (a pseudonym for E. P. Warren), *A Defence of Uranian Love* (London: 1928–1930), and the same writer's novel *A Tale of Pausanian Love* (London: 1927); in both of these the *Symposium* makes prominent appearances.

(p. 237), is set against the physicality of Maurice and the game-keeper, Alec, which will be expressed away from England ("an exile they gladly embrace"). *Maurice* might indeed be seen as a meditation on Carpenter's observation, confirmed by generations of independent witnesses, that "lust and love—the *Aphrodite Pandemos* and the *Aphrodite Ouranios*—are subtly interchangeable."[6]

It is, of course, not just Pausanias whose account found later admirers. The Uranian novel of F. W. Rolfe (Baron Corvo), *The Desire and Pursuit of the Whole* (published in 1934, more than twenty years after Rolfe's death), which is (in part) the story of the relationship in Venice between an Englishman and a teenage girl, "straight-limbed, and strong, almost as sexless as a boy, white as milk and honey" (pp. 8–9), takes its title and its opening and closing frame from the Platonic Aristophanes, whose myth, as we have already noted (above, p. 67), has exercised a strong fascination during various modern periods. Thus, anyone familiar with the *Symposium* will recognize the intellectual background to the following summary of part of the theory of desire of one of the great figures of twentieth-century psychoanalysis, Jacques Lacan:

> To make matters worse, Lacan announces, a fundamental Freudian insight is suppressed by the theoretical over-promoters of need. . . . Something else is always going on in dealings between the need-driven subject and the other who may or may not provide satisfaction. A demand for love is being made. The divided subject, haunted by absence and lack, looks to the other not simply to supply his needs but to pay him the compliment of an unconditional *yes*. . . . The paradox and the perversity to be found in any recourse to persons is that the other to whom the appeal is addressed is never in a position to answer it unconditionally. He too is divided and haunted, and his *yes*, however loudly it is proclaimed, can only ever be a *maybe*, or a *to some extent*, in disguise.
>
> Desire has its origin in this non-adequation between need and the demand for love, and in the equally grave dis-

[6] Carpenter (1923) 16.

crepancy between the demand itself and the addressee's ability to deliver.[7]

Here again our apparent dissatisfaction with sexual "satisfaction," the fact that *erôs* is not the same thing as physical need, is what is central, as it was for the Platonic Aristophanes. Lacan recurred explicitly on a number of occasions to Aristophanes' myth as a possible, though inadequate, model for "desire" (as he understood it).[8] For Lacan, desire, like language, never reaches "the happy end" that Aristophanes holds out as a possibility: one displacement, one metonymy, always leads to another: "[Desire] is a dimension in which the subject is always destined to travel too far or not far enough . . . and in which each anticipated moment of plenitude brings with it a new vacancy."[9] Aristophanes' myth had in fact already more than once caught the attention of Sigmund Freud, the great predecessor with whom Lacan is in constant dialogue. In *Beyond the Pleasure Principle*, Freud uses the story of the double-people as the starting point for some speculation:

> Shall we follow the hint given us by the poet-philosopher [the Platonic Aristophanes], and venture upon the hypothesis that living substance at the time of its coming to life was torn apart into small particles, which have ever since endeavoured to reunite through the sexual instincts? that these instincts, in which the chemical affinity of inanimate matter persisted, gradually succeeded, as they developed through the kingdom of the protista, in overcoming the difficulties put in the way of that endeavour by an environment charged with dangerous stimuli—stimuli which compelled them to form a protective cortical layer? that these splintered fragments of living substance in this way attained a multicellular condition and finally transferred the instinct for reuniting, in the most highly concentrated form, to the

[7] Bowie (1991) 135–36.
[8] Cf. Lacan (1977b) index, s.v. "Plato."
[9] Bowie (1991) 137–38.

germ-cells?—But here, I think, the moment has come for breaking off.[10]

Plato's Aristophanes thus becomes an early cell physiologist, but it is appropriate to that character's comic powers that Freud's speculations may also suggest the searching sperm of Woody Allen's *Everything You Ever Wanted to Know about Sex.*[11]

Lacan also found cause for reflection in Alcibiades' narrative, and here (as always) his reading is very much his own:

> Included in the *objet* a [i.e., the object of erotic fantasy, the "*autre*"] is the ἄγαλμα (*agalma*), the inestimable treasure that Alcibiades declares is contained in the rustic box that for him Socrates's face represents. But let us observe that it bears the sign (-) [i.e., absence of the phallic image]. It is because he has not seen Socrates's prick,[12] if I may be permitted to follow Plato, who does not spare us the details, that Alcibiades the seducer exalts in him the ἄγαλμα, the marvel that he would like Socrates to cede to him in avowing his desire: the division of the subject that he bears within himself being admitted with great clarity on this occasion. . . .
>
> Thus by showing his object as castrated, Alcibiades presents himself as he who desires—a fact that does not escape Socrates's attention—for someone else who is present, Agathon, whom Socrates, the precursor of psychoanalysis, and confident of his position in this fashionable gathering, does not hesitate to name as the object of the transference, placing in the light of an interpretation a fact that many analysts are still unaware of: that the love-hate effect in the analytic situation is to be found elsewhere.
>
> But Alcibiades is certainly not a neurotic. It is even because he is *par excellence* he who desires, and he who goes as

---

[10] Freud (1961) 52.

[11] The animation sequences in *Hedwig and the Angry Inch* (above, p. 67) also use both searching sperm and the splitting and recombining of cells to illustrate the ideas of Aristophanes' speech from the *Symposium.*

[12] The literal-minded may think this improbable after all that naked wrestling.

far as he can along the path of *jouissance*, that he can thus (with the help of a certain amount of drink) produce in the eyes of all the central articulation of the transference, made present by the object adorned with his reflexions.

Nevertheless, he projected Socrates into the ideal of the perfect Master, whom, through the action of (−Φ) [i.e., the phallic image], he has completely imaginarized.[13]

The temptation to see Lacan here entering into the spirit of sympotic self-parody is perhaps to be resisted. There is in fact no better witness to the power of Plato's vivid prose than this extraordinary attempt to get behind his characters and write their hidden lives. Many lay readers of Plato's dialogues would, however, testify to the fact that psychological insight,[14] understood in a far less technical way, is indeed an important facet of his Socrates, and the Lacanian gloss is a sophisticated attempt (one among many) to articulate what is a widespread admiration.

That reading the *Symposium*, with whatever degree of historical sophistication, can change one's life is attested, for example, on the first page of *Sex and Reason*, a 1992 study of the history of the relations between law and sexual behavior by R. A. Posner, a U.S. Federal Appeals Court judge:

> Two events . . . set me on the research path that has culminated in this book. The first was an attempt to plug one of many embarrassing gaps in my education by reading Plato's *Symposium*. I knew it was about love, but that was all I knew. I was surprised to discover that it was a defense, and as one can imagine a highly interesting and articulate one, of homosexual love. It had never occurred to me that the greatest figure in the history of philosophy, or for that matter any other respectable figure in the history of thought, had attempted such a thing. It dawned on me that the discussion

---

[13] Lacan (1977a) 322–23.

[14] Lear (1998) 162–66 discusses the fundamental differences between the aims of psychoanalysis and the philosophical ascent described by Diotima.

of the topic in the opinions in *Bowers v. Hardwick* [the decision in which the Supreme Court in 1986 upheld the constitutionality of state laws criminalizing homosexual sodomy] was superficial, although that did not mean the decision was incorrect. The second event was the decision of my own court to hear . . . a case involving the constitutionality of a state statute that had been interpreted to forbid striptease dancers to strip to the buff. Unusually for our court, the case generated fifty-three dense pages in the *Federal Reporter*. (The decision by the Supreme Court, reversing our 7–4 decision by a 5–4 vote, generated four opinions—none of which commanded the support of a majority of the justices.) It will be apparent to anyone who takes the trouble to read these opinions that nudity and the erotic are emotional topics even to middle-aged men and elderly judges and also that the dominant judicial, and I would say legal, attitude toward the study of sex is that "I know what I like" and therefore research is superfluous.[15]

Whether Plato would have welcomed the description of the *Symposium* as "the first document of sexology"[16] may be doubted (and he probably had little time for female strippers), but Greek intellectuals more generally would have welcomed in Posner another convert to the fold of a historicizing approach to questions of "nature" and "custom."

For those with a different agenda, of course, the very same features of the *Symposium* which had opened Judge Posner's eyes make the work utterly abhorrent. Thus, for example, the great Jewish intellectual Philo of Alexandria (late first century BC–early first century AD), who was steeped in Plato and knew the *Symposium* well, can represent its promotion of pederasty, which for Philo is contrary to "nature,"[17] as the cause of "the end of civilisation as we

[15] Posner (1992) 1–2; also cited in part by Nussbaum (1994) 1516–17.

[16] Posner (1992) 13.

[17] For such attitudes in Greek, rather than Jewish, tradition, cf. Goldhill (1995) chapter 2.

know it." He is writing in praise of a community of Jewish ascetics and contrasts their way of life with the banquets of Greece:

> The chief part [of the *Symposium*] is taken up by the common vulgar (*pandêmos*) love which takes away the courage (*andreia*) which is the virtue most valuable for the life both of peace and war, sets up the disease of effeminacy in their souls and turns into a hybrid of man and woman (*androgynoi*) those who should have been disciplined in all the practices which make for valour. And having wrought havoc with the years of boyhood and reduced the boy to the grade and condition of a girl besieged by a lover (lit. of a female *erômenos*) it inflicts damage on the lovers also in three most essential respects, their bodies, their souls and their property. . . . As a side growth we have another greater evil which affects all the people (*pandêmos*). Cities are desolated, the best kind of men become scarce, sterility and childlessness ensue through the devices of these who imitate men who have no knowledge of husbandry by sowing not in the deep soil of the lowland but in briny fields and stony and stubborn places, which not only give no possibility for anything to grow but even destroy the seed deposited within them.[18] I pass over the mythical stories of the double-bodied men. . . . these are seductive enough, calculated by the novelty of the notion to beguile the ear, but the disciples of Moses trained from their earliest years to love the truth regard them with supreme contempt and continue undeceived. (Philo, *De vita contemplativa* 7.60−63; trans. F. H. Colson, adapted)

For Pausanias, of course, it was *heterosexual* relations which came under *pandêmos erôs*; the *andreia* instilled by pederasty was praised (in their different ways) by Phaedrus (178d−79a), Aristophanes (192a4−5), and Agathon (196c−d), and the *androgynoi* of the *Symposium* were

---

[18] As commentators note, Plato himself has the "Athenian stranger" describe male homosexual intercourse with this same image at *Laws* 8.838e−39a. For an even stronger Philonic attack on homosexuality, but one sharing many of the same terms and images as the passage quoted, cf. *Spec. Leg.* 3.37−42.

the male-female creatures of Aristophanes' myth (189e2, 191d7), not "womanly men" (which is the standard sense of the Greek term); Philo here turns the language of Plato's work on its head to make his point about Greek decadence. Such moralizing has, of course, no monopoly on misrepresentation. In Achilles Tatius's novel (second century AD), a pederast and a committed heterosexual, both of whom have interests firmly rooted in the physical, argue about whether boys or women are more "heavenly" (*ouranios*; Ach. Tat. 2.36–38).

The middle course in these debates has always been steered by those who admire Plato and the Greek achievement but feel the need to apologize for and/or explain away the apparent promotion of homosexuality. Many such apologies, as indeed do other, more scholarly explanations, trace in Greek homosexuality an outlet for emotions whose "natural" path was blocked by the low status of women. Thus, for example, immediately after translating the *Symposium* in 1818, Shelley composed what amounted to an introductory essay to the translation, "Discourse on the Manners of the Antient Greeks relative to the Subject of Love";[19] for Shelley, who saw in the partial advancement of the position of women[20] and the parallel abolition of slavery "the most decisive [improvement] in the regulation of human society" to be put down to the credit of "modern Europeans," the explanation for Greek homosexuality lay precisely in the position of women, who are in principle "the legitimate object" of sentimental passion. Women had, said Shelley, been reduced to the position of slaves, and the result was inevitable:

> The women, thus degraded, became such as it was expected that they should become. They possessed, except with extraordinary exceptions, the habits and qualities of slaves. They were probably not extremely beautiful; at least there was no such disproportion in the attractions of the external form

[19] The translation and the "Discourse" are published together in a volume edited by R. Ingpen (London: 1931).

[20] Shelley knew that there was a long way to go and has strong words about the failure of his own society to abolish "totally" the inferior position of women (16).

between the female and male sex among the Greeks, as exists among the modern Europeans. They were certainly devoid of that moral and intellectual loveliness with which the acquisition of knowledge and the cultivation of sentiment animates, as with another life of overpowering grace, the lineaments and the gestures of every form which it inhabits. Their eyes could not have been deep and intricate from the workings of the mind, and could have entangled no heart in soul-enwoven labyrinths. (Shelley, "Discourse" 9–10)

Both the ancient Greeks and the "modern Europeans" had arrived "at that epoch of refinement, when sentimental love becomes an imperious want of the heart and of the mind," but only in modern times has the improvement in the position of women meant that both "the sexual and intellectual claims of love" can be satisfied in one union with "no gross violation in the established nature of man." When it comes to the physical details which lay behind the high Greek ideals, Shelley is more restrained than some modern researchers into Greek sexual practices: "We are not exactly aware, — and the laws of modern composition scarcely permit a modest writer to investigate the subject with philosophical accuracy, — what the action was by which the Greeks expressed this passion [of man for man]." Nevertheless, whether it imagined celibate high-mindedness or occasional anal intercourse as the Greek norm, Shelley reminded his own society that it had no cause for self-satisfaction, when it considered the horrors "endured by almost every youth of England with a diseased and insensate prostitute." Shelley's gaze upon Otherness seems indeed almost Herodotean:

Nothing is at the same time more melancholy and ludicrous than to observe that the inhabitants of one epoch, or of one nation, harden themselves to all amelioration of their own practices and institutions and soothe their consciences by heaping violent invectives upon those of others; while in the eye of sane philosophy their own are none the less deserving of censure. (Shelley, "Discourse" 17)

The past is, of course, always contested, never more so than when it is used to justify our own patterns of behavior. In 1993, passages of both the *Symposium* and the *Laws* were expounded and argued about in a Colorado court, which had to decide the legality of a state constitutional amendment forbidding any state agency from designating any form of gay or bisexual "orientation, conduct, practices, or relationships" as a basis for protected legal status.[21] At issue between the expert witnesses summoned by both sides of the case was whether there was indeed a strong non-Christian tradition in the West which regarded gay sex as unnatural and immoral. Opponents of the amendment won.

2 | Sympotic Revisions

Echoes of and allusions to the *Symposium* are legion in antiquity, particularly from the period of the so-called Second Sophistic, a brilliant flowering of Greek culture in the Roman Empire of the late first and second centuries AD. At the heart of this culture was a rethinking, and indeed often reliving, of the classical past through its great texts and monuments. Plato played a central role in this life of the imagination. Thus, for example, Plutarch's *Erôtikos* (or *Amatorius*) is the record of conversations between Plutarch and his friends at a Boeotian festival for Eros and the Muses; the part of Plato's Apollodorus is played by Plutarch's son, who seems to have memorized a very full account of what went on at the festival. The work, littered with verbal echoes of Plato, combines ideas taken from the *Symposium* and the *Phaedrus* with a quite un-Platonic narrative of a local woman's passion for a younger man.[22] As frequently in the Second Sophistic, a central structuring opposition, again traceable to Plato's Pausanias, is a debate about the relative merits of

[21] Cf. Clark (2000). For the views of the competing authorities, cf. Nussbaum (1994); Finnis (1994).
[22] Cf. Rist (2001).

loving women and boys. In this same period, at least one (now lost) commentary on the *Symposium* was written.[23]

As we have already noted, the *Symposium* became the foundational text for all literary dinner parties which followed. Among its most famous progeny is the dinner party of Trimalchio which forms the centerpiece of our surviving extracts of Petronius's *Satyrica* (first century AD). At this party, the obsession of the host and guests with the quality of food and drink reverses the intellectual fare on which Agathon's guests feed, but the entry of Trimalchio's friend, the stonemason Habinnas, obviously reworks the entry of Alcibiades to Agathon's party:[24]

> Meanwhile, an official's attendant knocked on the dining room doors and a reveller (*comissator*) dressed in white came in trailing a large crowd of followers. . . . He was already drunk and ploughed along after his wife with his hands propped on her shoulders. A bunch of wreaths were piled on his head and scented oil streamed down his forehead into his eyes. He sat down in the seat of honour and immediately called for wine and hot water. Charmed by his high spirits, Trimalchio ordered a larger bowl of wine for himself, and asked how his friend had been entertained at another party. "We had it all—except for you," he said. (Petronius, *Satyrica* 65.3−9; trans. Branham and Kinney)

The narrator of the *Satyrica*, Encolpius, is addicted to seeing, in his own life, patterns familiar from the great literature of the past: if, then, he is at a dinner party, there has to be an "Alcibiades." The *Satyrica* as a whole is the story of the adventures of Encolpius and

---

[23] Significant parts of the same unknown author's commentary on the *Theaetetus* survive; cf. *Corpus dei Papiri Filosofici Greci e Latini* III (Florence: 1995); for the *Symposium* commentary, cf. pp. 454−55, col. LXX 10−12.

[24] Cf. Cameron (1969). More generally on Petronius's use of the *Symposium*, cf. Dupont (1977); Bessone (1993), with further bibliography. Alcibiades also enters drunk in Iris Murdoch's "Above the Gods," the second "Platonic" dialogue in *Acastos* (London: 1986).

his promiscuous boyfriend, Giton, a pairing which is entirely carnal, but out of which Encolpius fantasizes higher romance. It would be easy enough to see this lowlife narrative as a satire on the high educational pretensions of, say, Pausanias's speech in the *Symposium*, though the most lovable hypocrite in the work is not in fact Encolpius, but rather Eumolpus, a lecherous poet and "educator" whose famous story of "the Pergamene boy" brilliantly replays Alcibiades' narrative of his night with Socrates.[25] Eumolpus tells how, by pretending to be a stern moralist scandalized by any mention of pederasty, he was allowed unfettered access to the handsome son of his hosts at Pergamum. While the boy appears to sleep, Eumolpus performs a series of increasingly intimate physical acts with him; the boy, however, is far from unaware of what is happening and proves in the end so insatiable for sex that it is Eumolpus who has finally to repeat the punch line that we have already had from the molested youth: "Go to sleep, or I'll tell father!" The story ironizes Pausanias's account of the attitudes of an *erastês* and an *erômenos* toward their roles in an ideal relationship by exploiting the idea of the straightforward "exchange"—sex for wisdom—which Alcibiades offered Socrates and in which Socrates seemed to have so little interest.

The *Satyrica* is often seen as, in part, a parodic inversion of the pattern of narrative best illustrated, though with significant differences, by the extant Greek novels (all probably later in date than Petronius) of Chariton, Xenophon of Ephesus, Achilles Tatius, and Heliodorus: a heterosexual pair of lovers is separated and endures incredible adventures and threats to their chastity, but they remain faithful to each other until they are finally reunited. Such a plot, driven by the single-minded obsession with each other of a pair of lovers, an obsessive search to fill the hole left by the beloved's disappearance, seems to find an archetype not just in the travails of Odysseus and Penelope, but also in Aristophanes' story in the *Symposium* of the double-people and our constant search for our other half. Achilles Tatius in fact uses a distorted echo of this myth for a

---

[25] Cf. Hunter (1996) 200–204 for a fuller discussion.

very particular effect at the beginning of his work. The principal narrator, Clitophon, is speaking about his father's intention to marry him to his half sister Calligone:

> When I was in my nineteenth year, and my father was preparing to celebrate our nuptials the following year, Fortune set the drama in motion. I had a dream in which my lower parts were fused up to the navel with those of my bride, while from there we had separate upper bodies. A huge, terrifying woman with a savage countenance appeared: her eyes were bloodshot, her cheeks rugged, and her hair made of snakes. She was wielding a sickle in her right hand, and a torch in the other. This creature attacked me with furious passion: raising her sickle she brought it down on my loins, where the two bodies were joined, and lopped off my bride. (Ach. Tat. 1.3.3−4; trans. T. Whitmarsh)

Readers who know their *Symposium*, and for Achilles that means all implied readers, will recognize that the systematic distortion of the Platonic text—here a Siamese twins effect, there complete union, here a chthonic Fury with a sickle, there the Olympians with their more precise tools, here a nightmare, there a dreamlike wish fulfillment of perfect bodily union—strongly suggests that Calligone is not Clitophon's "other half" in the Aristophanic sense; and so it is to prove.

Another novel which parades its links with the *Symposium* is Apuleius's *Metamorphoses* (or *The Golden Ass*), the tale of a man called Lucius, whose curiosity about magical practice leads to his transformation into an ass; after many sordid adventures, he is returned to human shape by the intervention of the great goddess Isis, whose priest he becomes. Within this picaresque narrative, characters tell many amusing tales of the kind which look forward to Chaucer and Boccaccio, and the middle of the novel is occupied by the inserted tale of Cupid's love for Psyche (Soul), her search for him and the labors she must endure, and her final ascent to Olympus to be united with him. "Cupid and Psyche" has clear Platonic elements, taken most notably from the *Phaedrus* and from Diotima's speech in the *Symposium*, and it is also plainly an allegory of the soul's search for higher reality. Moreover, it also offers at one level an allegorical interpretation of the story of Lucius's fall to asshood and subsequent recovery which frames it, and this interpretation depends upon a distinction between "carnal" pleasures, which led Lucius astray and with which the world of the novel is overly full, and "higher" love, such as both Psyche and Lucius ultimately obtain; this dichotomy may be traced back to Pausanias's speech in the *Symposium*, to where we may perhaps also trace the very notion of a duality of love in pagan and Christian traditions.[26] Plato had, moreover, shown the way structurally as well as thematically. Thus Diotima's speech (particularly the myth of Eros's birth) may similarly be read not merely as itself an allegory requiring interpretation, but also as an allegorical interpretation of the (very physical) narrative of Alcibiades' relations with Socrates which immediately follows it. Where Plato led, Apuleius (as so often) followed.

The *Symposium* is indeed a classic text for the history of interpretation: Alcibiades' image of Socrates and his words as a Silenus who needs to be "opened up" to reveal "the divine things" inside has proved, as we have already noted (above, pp. 11–12), to be a productive way of imaging critical interpretation, which has found notable imitators. Central to the interpretive practices, both pagan and Christian, of later antiquity and the Byzantine period is the fact that a text, an idea, or a concept (such as *erôs*) may be understood at various levels, which can often be represented as of increasing complexity and sophistication, from the literal "rising upward" to the richly allegorical. Even when the pattern of the *Symposium* is not explicitly invoked by later authors, its influence may be felt all over the voluminous theological and scholastic writing of these periods. Those wishing to create Platonic authority for their own interpretive practices may be tempted to find in the series of encomia of *erôs* in the *Symposium* an ever-increasing level of sophistication, culminating in the speech of Socrates/Diotima, and such an "ascent" in the pattern of the speeches then finds its analogy in the ascent of the

---

[26] For the *Symposium* and Christian theology, cf. Rist (1964); Osborne (1994).

soul within the speech of Socrates/Diotima itself. Thus as a text which itself requires interpretation, which contains models and patterns of interpretation within it (Diotima's allegory, Alcibiades' Silenus image, the idea of higher understanding as a "mystery"), and which, through the succession of different understandings of *erôs*, gives structural embodiment to the process of interpretation as a series of stages of increasing sophistication and complexity, the *Symposium* was determinative of the way in which classical and Christian texts, including of course Plato himself, were read. More broadly, in its mixture of interconnectedness and fragmentation, its provocative challenge to fit the parts into a whole, and our constant need to reevaluate what we have already read in the light of the subsequent speeches, the *Symposium* both reproduces and shapes the very practice of critical interpretation, if not indeed of reading itself.

Diotima's myth is, of course, one of the most discussed and interpreted parts of the *Symposium*; her own seerlike status and her quasi-mystical language of psychic pregnancy and "giving birth in the beautiful" were an irresistible provocation to those who ceaselessly harried the Platonic text to find the metaphysical truth. Her teaching about *daimones* which mediate between gods and men was extremely influential in the later Platonic traditions; Apuleius's *On the God of Socrates* is a prime example.[27] Plotinus (third century AD), the most important of the neo-Platonists, expounded Diotima's myth of the birth of Eros at least three times, including a full-scale exposition in the essay "On *Erôs*" (*Ennead* 3.5).[28] In this reading the heavenly Aphrodite is Soul, and her father, Kronos, is Intellect (*nous*); the following extract gives a fair flavor of the interpretation:

> Plenty (i.e., Poros), then, since he is a rational principle in the intelligible world and in Intellect, and since he is more diffused and, as it were, spread out, would be concerned with soul and in soul. For that which is in Intellect is contracted together, and nothing comes to it from anything else,

[27] This is most accessible in Harrison, Hilton, and Hunink (2001).

[28] Cf. Dillon (1969); Osborne (1994) 112–14. For Plotinus's other interpretations, cf. *Enn.* 3.6.14, 6.9.9.

but when Plenty was drunk his state of being filled was brought about from outside. But what could that which is filled with nectar in the higher world be except a rational principle which has fallen from a higher origin to a lesser one? So this principle is in Soul and comes from Intellect, flowing into his garden when Aphrodite is said to have been born. And every garden is a glory and decoration of wealth; and the property of Zeus is glorified by rational principle, and his decorations are the glories that come from Intellect itself into the soul. Or what could the garden of Zeus be but his images in which he takes delight and his glories? And what could his glories and adornments be but the rational principles which flow from him? The rational principles all together are Plenty, the plenitude and wealth of beauties, already manifested; and this is the being drunk with nectar. For what is nectar for the gods but that which the divinity acquires? (Plotinus, *Ennead* 3.5.9; trans. A. H. Armstrong)

Plato, perhaps, had only himself to blame: never had the invitation to interpretation which the *Symposium* playfully holds out been embraced with such enthusiasm.

Not, of course, that Plotinus was the first to have struck out along this path. Plotinus explicitly cites, in order to reject, an interpretation which made Diotima's Eros stand for the universe (*kosmos*); an instance of such a reading is preserved in Plutarch's essay *On Isis and Osiris*, which seeks to harmonize Greek and Egyptian speculation about the origins of the world:

This subject seems in some wise to call up the myth of Plato, which Socrates in the *Symposium* gives at some length in regard to the birth of Love, saying that Poverty, wishing for children, insinuated herself beside Plenty while he was asleep, and having become pregnant by him, gave birth to Love, who is of a mixed and utterly variable nature, inasmuch as he is the son of a father who is good and wise and self-sufficient in all things, but of a mother who is helpless and without means and because of want always clinging close to another and always importunate over another. For Plenty is none other than the first beloved and desired, the perfect and self-sufficient; and Plato calls raw material Poverty, utterly lacking of herself in the Good, but being filled from him and always yearning for him and sharing with him. The World (*kosmos*), or Horus, which is born of these, is not eternal nor unaffected nor imperishable, but, being ever reborn, contrives to remain always young and never subject to destruction in the changes and cycles of events. (Plutarch, *On Isis and Osiris* 374c–e; trans. F. C. Babbitt)

Christianity was also to claim a privileged place in the history of such mystical readings of Platonic texts. Very few reworkings of the *Symposium* are as remarkable as the *Symposium* of the Lycian bishop Methodius (second half of third century AD), in which ten Christian virgins deliver encomia of Virginity (*parthenia*, here etymologized, in a manner familiar to readers of Plato's *Cratylus*, as *partheia*, nearness to god). The host is no longer the Platonic "Mr. Good," but rather Arete (Virtue), daughter of Philosophia, and Socrates is replaced by Saint Thecla, a "martyr" like her classical predecessor, whose speech contains large elements from both Diotima in Plato's *Symposium* and the mystic Socrates of the *Phaedrus*.[29] The high point of Christian readings of the *Symposium* is, however, the commentary upon this work by the great Florentine humanist and philosopher Marsilio Ficino (1433–1499), whose life work included translating into Latin all of Plato and Plotinus. Under the patronage of Cosimo de' Medici, Ficino was at the center of a Florentine "Academy" devoted to the celebration and exposition of Platonic philosophy. His commentary on the *Symposium* (1469) is as dramatic in its structure as the text on which it comments; here is the opening in which Ficino explains its origins:

Plato, the father of philosophers, passed away at the age of eighty-one after the food had been cleared away at a banquet

[29] English translation is in Musurillo (1958); for discussion cf. Brown (1988) 183–89.

on his birthday, November 7. This banquet, which commemorated both his birthday and the anniversary of his death, was renewed every year by all the early Platonists down to the time of Plotinus and Porphyry. But for twelve hundred years after Porphyry these annual feasts were not observed. At last in our own day, the illustrious Lorenzo de' Medici, wishing to reestablish the Platonic symposium, appointed Francesco Bandini Master of the Feast and so, when Bandini had declared November 7 the date for the celebration, he entertained in regal splendour at the villa, at Careggio,[30] nine guest Platonists: Antonio Agli, Bishop of Fiesole; Ficino, the physician [Marsilio's father]; Cristoforo Landino, the poet; Bernardo Nuzzi, the rhetorician; Tommaso Benci; Giovanni Cavalcanti, our dear friend, whom because of his virtue of soul and noble appearance, they named Hero of the feast; the two Marsuppini, Cristoforo and Carlo, sons of the poet Carlo Marsuppini; and finally, Bandini wished me to be the ninth, so that with the addition of the name Marsilio Ficino to those already mentioned, the number of the Muses might be rounded out.

When the food had been cleared away, Bernardo Nuzzi took the volume of Plato which is inscribed *Symposium on Love* and read all the speeches of this *Symposium*. When he had finished reading, he asked that each of the guests explain one of the speeches. They all consented, and when the lots had been drawn, the first speech, that of Phaedrus, fell to Giovanni Cavalcanti to explain. The speech of Pausanias fell to the theologian Agli; that of Eryximachus, the physician, to the physician Ficino; that of the poet Aristophanes to the poet Landino; that of Agathon, the young man, to Carlo Marsuppini; to Tommaso Benci was given the discourse of Socrates, and finally the speech of Alcibiades fell to Cristoforo Marsuppini. Everyone approved the lot as it

---

[30] A town on the hills outside Florence where Cosimo had given Ficino a house.

had fallen out; but the bishop and the physician were called away, the one to the care of souls, the other to the care of bodies, and they resigned their parts to Giovanni Cavalcanti, to whom the rest then turned and fell silent, ready to listen. (trans. S. R. Jayne)[31]

For us, Renaissance Florence seems another brilliant society which appeals, like classical Athens, as much to our imagination as to our historical sense; Ficino's narrative encloses that brilliance within a single space, just as did Plato's. In replaying the *Symposium*, but at the level of interpretation, Bandini's guests move a further step beyond the role playing which is already inherent in Plato's text (above, p. 10); as their speeches interpret the speeches which Plato had put into the mouths of Agathon and his guests, so Ficino himself plays Plato, for he is of course the real author of the speeches which fill the commentary.

Just as it was accepted that Plato had revealed some of his greatest mystic truths in this work, so Ficino lays out in the commentary a Christianizing vision of metaphysical "Platonic love" in which love between human souls is secured by their love for God, the supreme principle of Beauty and Goodness, and God's love for them. The whole hierarchy of structures in God's world is illumined and kept in harmonious balance by Love: God is at the center of four circles—Mind (associated with the "Heavenly Venus"), Soul (associated with the generative power of Venus, daughter of Jupiter and Dione), Nature, and Matter—which, being derived from God, are always turned toward him by Love and forever strive to return to him. Ficino, like Diotima before him, appropriates Pausanias's duality of Aphrodite for a vision in which *all* Love, if properly respected (physical sex between men was, of course, "unnatural"), serves higher purposes:

> Venus is two-fold: one is clearly that intelligence which we said was in the Angelic Mind; the other is the power of gen-

[31] S. R. Jayne, *Marsilio Ficino's Commentary on Plato's Symposium* (Columbia, Miss.: 1944).

eration with which the World-Soul is endowed. Each has as consort a similar Love. The first, by innate love is stimulated to know the beauty of God; the second, by its love, to procreate the same beauty in bodies. The former Venus first embraces the Glory of God in herself, and then translates it to the second Venus. This latter Venus translates sparks of that divine glory into earthly matter. It is because of sparks of this kind that an individual body seems beautiful to us, in proportion to its merits. The human soul perceives the beauty of these bodies through the eyes.

The soul also has two powers. It certainly has the power of comprehension, and it has the power of generation. These two powers in us are the two Venuses which are accompanied by their twin Loves. When the beauty of a human body first meets our eyes, the mind, which is the first Venus in us, worships and adores the human beauty as an image of divine beauty, and through the first, it is frequently aroused to the second. But the power of generation in us, which is the second Venus, desires to create another form like this. Therefore, there is a Love in each case: in the former, it is the desire of contemplating Beauty; and in the latter, the desire for propagating it; both loves are honorable and praiseworthy, for each is concerned with the divine image. (*Commentary on the Symposium*, second speech, chap. 7; trans. S. R. Jayne)

Through Ficino and his followers, the mystical ideas of the *Phaedrus* and the *Symposium* exercised enormous influence upon subsequent literature, thought, and art.[32] Our postmodern world is suspicious of all-encompassing systems, particularly ones which could easily be parodied as New Age babble *avant la lettre*, but this should not blind us to the power of an intellectual conception which combined the most haunting texts of exploratory pagan philosophy with the confirming strength of a revealed and certain truth.

[32] Cf., e.g., Festugière (1941).

Bibliography and Further Reading

There are many readily available translations of the *Symposium*. Particularly recommended are that of Robin Waterfield in the Oxford World's Classics series (1994), which has been used in this book, and that of A. Nehamas and P. Woodruff (Indianapolis, Ind.: Hackett, 1989). Rowe (1998) offers a Greek text, facing English translation, and very helpful notes in which virtually all Greek is transliterated.

There is a convenient and brief account of the classical Athenian symposium in Davidson (1997); much of the large bibliography on this subject can be traced through Murray (1990a) and Slater (1991); the best introduction to the rich iconography of the Greek symposium is Lissarrague (1990). For the place of poetry in the symposium, Gentili (1988), Stehle (1997), and Ford (2002) offer interesting and reliable guides.

Calame (1992) offers an introduction to the whole range of issues connected with the literary representation of *erôs*. On homosexual relations in Greek antiquity the classic study is Dover (1978), and see now Hubbard (2003) for a collection of sources in translation; a useful overview of work since Dover can be traced through the notes of Hubbard (1998). Halperin (1990), the second chapter of Winkler (1990), and chapter 7 of Cohen (1991) raise particularly important considerations.

The following lists all works cited by short title in the notes and guidance offered above, together with certain other works which will help those who wish to pursue these subjects further.

Bacon, H. H. 1959. "Socrates crowned" *Virginia Quarterly Review* 35: 415–30.

Barthes, R. 1978. *A Lover's Discourse: Fragments* (trans. R. Howard), New York.

Bessone, F. 1993. "Discorsi dei liberti e parodia del 'Simposio' platonico nella 'Cena Trimalchionis'" *Materiali e Discussioni* 30: 63–86.

Blondell, R. 2002. *The Play of Character in Plato's Dialogues*, Cambridge.

Bowie, A. M. 1997. "Thinking with drinking: wine and the symposium in Aristophanes" *Journal of Hellenic Studies* 117: 1–21.

Bowie, M. 1991. *Lacan*, Cambridge, Mass.

Brown, P. 1988. *The Body and Society*, New York/London.

Burkert, W. 1985. *Greek Religion*, Oxford.

Burnyeat, M. F. 1977. "Socratic midwifery, Platonic inspiration" *Bulletin of the Institute of Classical Studies* 24: 7–16.

Bury, R. G. 1932. *The Symposium of Plato*, 2^d ed., Cambridge.

Calame, C. 1992. *The Poetics of Eros in Ancient Greece*, Princeton, N.J.

Cameron, A. 1969. "Petronius and Plato" *Classical Quarterly* 19: 367–70.

Carpenter, E. 1923. *Love's Coming-of-Age*, 12th ed., London.

Clark, R. B. 2000. "Platonic love in a Colorado courtroom: Martha Nussbaum, John Finnis, and Plato's *Laws* in *Evans v. Romer*" *Yale Journal of Law and the Humanities* 12: 1–38.

Clay, D. 1983. "The tragic and comic poet of the *Symposium*" in J. P. Anton and A. Preus (eds.), *Essays in Ancient Greek Philosophy*, Albany, N.Y., 186–202.

———. 1992. "Plato's first words" *Yale Classical Studies* 29: 113–29.

———. 2000. *Platonic Questions*, University Park, Pa.

Cohen, D. 1991. *Law, Sexuality, and Society*, Cambridge.

Davidson, J. 1997. *Courtesans and Fishcakes*, London.

———. 2000. "*Gnesippus paigniagraphos*: the comic poets and the erotic mime" in D. Harvey and J. Wilkins (eds.), *The Rivals of Aristophanes*, London, 41–64.

Dillon, J. 1969. "*Enn.* III 5: Plotinus' exegesis of the *Symposium* myth" ΑΓΩΝ 3: 24–44.

Dover, K. J. 1964. "Eros and nomos (Plato, *Symposium* 182A–185C)" *Bulletin of the Institute of Classical Studies* 11: 31–42.

———. 1965. "The date of Plato's *Symposium*" *Phronesis* 10: 2–20 (= Dover [1988] 86–101).

———. 1966. "Aristophanes' speech in Plato's *Symposium*" *Journal of Hellenic Studies* 86: 41–50 (= Dover [1988] 102–14).

———. 1968. *Aristophanes, Clouds*, Oxford.

———. 1974. *Greek Popular Morality in the Time of Plato and Aristotle*, Oxford.

———. 1978. *Greek Homosexuality*, London.

———. 1980. *Plato, Symposium*, Cambridge.

———. 1988. *The Greeks and Their Legacy*, Oxford.

———. 1997. *The Evolution of Greek Prose Style*, Oxford.

Dupont, F. 1977. *Le plaisir et la loi*, Paris.

Edelstein, L. 1945. "The role of Eryximachus in Plato's *Symposium*" *Transactions and Proceedings of the American Philological Association* 76: 85–103 (= *Ancient Medicine: Selected Papers of Ludwig Edelstein* [Baltimore, Md.: 1967] 153–71).

Ferrari, G. R. F. 1992. "Platonic love" in Kraut (1992) 248–76.

Ferrari, Gloria. 2002. *Figures of Speech*, Chicago, Ill.

Festugière, J. 1941. *La philosophie de l'amour de Marsile Ficin e son influence sur la littérature française au XVIe siècle*, Paris.

Finnis, J. M. 1994. "Law, morality, and 'sexual orientation'" *Notre Dame Law Review* 69: 1049–76.

Fisher, N. 2000. "Symposiasts, fish-eaters and flatterers: social mobility and moral concerns" in D. Harvey and J. Wilkins (eds.), *The Rivals of Aristophanes*, London, 355–96.

Ford, A. 2002. *The Origins of Criticism*, Princeton, N.J.

Forster, E. M. 1971. *Maurice*, London.

Foucault, M. 1985. *The Use of Pleasure*, New York.

Freud, S. 1961. *Beyond the Pleasure Principle* (trans. J. Strachey), 2d ed., London.

Gentili, B. 1988. *Poetry and Its Public in Ancient Greece*, Baltimore/London.

Goldhill, S. 1995. *Foucault's Virginity*, Cambridge.

Gribble, D. 1999. *Alcibiades and Athens*, Oxford.

Griffith, M. 2002. "Slaves of Dionysos: satyrs, audience, and the ends of the *Oresteia*" *Classical Antiquity* 21: 195–258.

Halperin, D. 1985. "Platonic *erôs* and what men call love" *Ancient Philosophy* 5: 161–204.

———. 1990. *One Hundred Years of Homosexuality*, New York/London.

———. 1992. "Plato and the erotics of narrativity" in J. C. Klagge and N. D. Smith (eds.), *Methods of Interpreting Plato and His Dialogues*, Oxford, 93–129.

Harrison, S., J. Hilton, and V. Hunink, 2001. *Apuleius, Rhetorical Works*, Oxford.

Henderson, J. 2000. "The life and soul of the party: Plato, *Symposium*" in A. Sharrock and H. Morales (eds.), *Intratextuality*, Oxford, 287–324.

————. forthcoming. "Anselm Feuerbach's *Das Gastmahl des Platon*" in M. B. Trapp (ed.), *Socrates in the Nineteenth and Twentieth Centuries*, Aldershot.

Hobbs, A. 2000. *Plato and the Hero*, Cambridge.

Hubbard, T. K. 1998. "Popular perceptions of elite homosexuality in classical Athens" *Arion* 6: 48–78.

————. 2003. *Homosexuality in Greece and Rome: A Sourcebook of Basic Documents*, Berkeley, Calif.

Hunter, R. 1996. "Response to J. Morgan" in A. H. Sommerstein and C. Atherton (eds.), *Education in Greek Fiction*, Bari, Italy, 191–205.

————. 2003. *Theocritus, Encomium of Ptolemy Philadelphus*, Berkeley, Calif.

Huss, B. 1999. *Xenophons Symposion: Ein Kommentar*, Stuttgart/Leipzig.

Janaway, C. 1995. *Images of Excellence*, Oxford.

Jenkyns, R. 1980. *The Victorians and Ancient Greece*, Oxford.

Johnson, W. A. 1998. "Dramatic frame and philosophic idea in Plato" *American Journal of Philology* 119: 577–98.

Jouanna, J. 1984. "Rhétorique et médecine dans la collection hippocratique" *Revue des Études Grecques* 9: 26–44.

Kahn, C. H. 1994. "Aeschines on Socratic eros" in P. A. Van der Waerdt (ed.), *The Socratic Movement*, Ithaca, N.Y./London, 87–106.

————. 1996. *Plato and the Socratic Dialogue*, Cambridge.

Konstan, D. 1994. *Sexual Symmetry*, Princeton, N.J.

Konstan, D., and E. Young-Bruehl. 1982. "Eryximachus' speech in the *Symposium*" *Apeiron* 16: 40–46.

Kraut, R. (ed.) 1992. *The Cambridge Companion to Plato*, Cambridge.

Lacan, J. 1977a. *Écrits: A Selection* (trans. A. Sheridan), London.

————. 1977b. *The Four Fundamental Concepts of Psychoanalysis* (trans. A. Sheridan), London.

Lear, J. 1998. *Open Minded*, Cambridge, Mass.

Lissarrague, F. 1990. *The Aesthetics of the Greek Banquet*, Princeton, N.J.

Lloyd, G. E. R. 1964. "The hot and the cold, the dry and the wet in Greek philosophy" *Journal of Hellenic Studies* 84: 92–106.

————. 1979. *Magic, Reason and Experience*, Cambridge.

Lowenstam, S. 1985. "Paradoxes in Plato's *Symposium*" *Ramus* 14: 85–104.

Ludwig, P. W. 2002. *Eros & Polis*, Cambridge.

McGrath, E. 1983. "'The drunken Alcibiades': Rubens's picture of Plato's *Symposium*" *Journal of the Courtauld and Warburg Institutes* 46: 228–35.

Macleod, C. 1981. "The comic encomium and Aristophanes, *Clouds* 1201 – 1211" *Phoenix* 35: 142–44 (= *Collected Essays* [Oxford: 1983] 49–51).

Martin, J. 1931. *Symposion: Die Geschichte einer literarischen Form*, Paderborn, Germany.

Mattingly, H. 1958. "The date of Plato's Symposium" *Phronesis* 3: 31–39.

Morrison, J. S. 1964. "Four notes on Plato's *Symposium*" *Classical Quarterly* 14: 42–55.

Murray, O. (ed.) 1990a. *Sympotica*, Oxford.

———. 1990b. "The affair of the Mysteries: democracy and the drinking group" in Murray (1990a) 149–61.

Musurillo, H. A. 1958. *Methodius, The Symposium*, London.

Nails, D. 2002. *The People of Plato*, Indianapolis, Ind.

Nehamas, A. 1998. *The Art of Living*, Berkeley, Calif.

Nightingale, A. 1995. *Genres in Dialogue*, Cambridge.

Nussbaum, M. 1986. *The Fragility of Goodness*, Cambridge.

———. 1994. "Platonic love and Colorado law: the relevance of ancient Greek norms to modern sexual controversies" *Virginia Law Review* 80: 1515–1651.

Osborne, C. 1994. *Eros Unveiled*, Oxford.

Patterson, R. 1982. "The Platonic art of comedy and tragedy" *Philosophy and Literature* 6: 76–93.

———. 1991. "The ascent in Plato's *Symposium*" *Proceedings of the Boston Area Colloquium in Ancient Philosophy* 7: 193–214.

Pender, E. 1992. "Spiritual pregnancy in Plato's *Symposium*" *Classical Quarterly* 42: 72–86.

Pirenne-Delforge, V. 1988. "Epithètes cultuelles et interprétation philosophique. À propos d'Aphrodite Ourania et Pandémos à Athènes" *L'Antiquité Classique* 57: 142–57.

Posner, R. A. 1992. *Sex and Reason*, Cambridge, Mass.

Price, A. W. 1989. *Love and Friendship in Plato and Aristotle*, Oxford.

Reckford, K. J. 1974. "Desire with hope: Aristophanes and the comic catharsis" *Ramus* 3: 41–69.

Riedweg, C. 1987. *Mysterienterminologie bei Platon, Philon und Klemens von Alexandrien*, Berlin/New York.

Riginos, A. S. 1976. *Platonica: The Anecdotes concerning the Life and Writings of Plato*, Leiden.

Rist, J. M. 1964. *Eros and Psyche*, Toronto.

———. 2001. "Plutarch's *Amatorius*: A commentary on Plato's theories of love?" *Classical Quarterly* 51: 557–75.

Rosen, S. 1987. *Plato's Symposium*, 2^d ed., New Haven, Conn./London.

Rowe, C. J. 1998. *Plato, Symposium*, Warminster.

———. 1999. "The speech of Eryximachus in Plato's *Symposium*" in J. J. Cleary (ed.), *Traditions of Platonism*, Aldershot, England, 53−64.

Rutherford, R. B. 1995. *The Art of Plato*, London.

Scott, D. 2000. "Socrates and Alcibiades in the *Symposium*" *Hermathena* 168: 25−37.

Sheffield, F. 2001a. "Psychic pregnancy and Platonic epistemology" *Oxford Studies in Ancient Philosophy* 20: 1−33.

———. 2001b. "Alcibiades' speech: a satyric drama" *Greece & Rome* 48: 193−209.

Sider, D. 1980. "Plato's *Symposium* as Dionysian festival" *Quaderni Urbinati di Cultura Classica* 33: 41−56.

Sier, K. 1997. *Die Rede der Diotima*, Stuttgart/Leipzig.

Slater, W. J. 1982. "Aristophanes of Byzantium and problem-solving in the Museum" *Classical Quarterly* 32: 336−49.

———. 1990. "Sympotic ethics in the *Odyssey*" in Murray (1990a) 213−20.

Slater, W. J. (ed.) 1991. *Dining in a Classical Context*, Ann Arbor.

Smith, T. d'A. 1970. *Love in Earnest*, London.

Stafford, E. 2000. *Worshipping Virtues*, London.

Stehle, E. 1997. *Performance and Gender in Ancient Greece*, Princeton, N.J.

Steiner, D. 1996. "For love of a statue: a reading of Plato's *Symposium* 215A−B" *Ramus* 25: 89−111.

———. 2001. *Images in Mind*, Princeton, N.J.

Stokes, M. C. 1986. *Plato's Socratic Conversations*, London.

Tecusan, M. 1990. "*Logos sympotikos*: patterns of the irrational in philosophical drinking: Plato outside the *Symposium*" in Murray (1990a) 238−60.

Thomas, R. 2000. *Herodotus in Context*, Cambridge.

———. 2003. "Prose performance texts: *epideixeis* and written publication in the late fifth and early fourth centuries" in H. Yunis (ed.), *Written Texts and the Rise of Literate Culture in Ancient Greece*, Cambridge, 162−88.

Usher, M. D. 2002. "Satyr play in Plato's *Symposium*" *American Journal of Philology* 123: 205−28.

Vlastos, G. 1973. *Platonic Studies*, Princeton, N.J.

———. 1991. *Socrates: Ironist and Moral Philosopher*, Cambridge.

Wardy, R. 2002. "The unity of opposites in Plato's *Symposium*" *Oxford Studies in Ancient Philosophy* 23: 1−61.

White, F. C. 1989. "Love and beauty in Plato's *Symposium*" *Journal of Hellenic Studies* 109: 149–57.

Wilkins, J. 2000. *The Boastful Chef*, Oxford.

Wilson, N. 1982. "Two observations on Aristophanes' *Lysistrata*" *Greek, Roman, and Byzantine Studies* 23: 157–63.

Wilson, P. 1999. "The *aulos* in Athens" in S. Goldhill and R. Osborne (eds.), *Performance Culture and Athenian Democracy*, Cambridge, 58–95.

Winkler, J. J. 1990. *The Constraints of Desire*, New York/London.

Wohl, V. 1999. "The eros of Alcibiades" *Classical Antiquity* 18: 349–85.

Zanker, P. 1995. *The Mask of Socrates*, Berkeley, Calif.

Index of Passages Discussed

Pages devoted to analysis of the individual speeches are marked in bold; not all references to passages within the speeches are noted separately.

Achilles Tatius
  Leucippe and Clitophon 1.3.3−4, 128
Alexis
  fr. 247 Kassel-Austin, 20
Amphis
  fr. 15 Kassel-Austin, 49−50
Aristophanes
  Clouds 365−411, 66
  Frogs 1425, 104
  Women at the Thesmophoria 39−265, 75−77
Athenaeus
  Sophists at Dinner 5.187c, 10

Hesiod
  Theogony 120−2, 40
Homer
  Odyssey 8.265−366, 8−9
  9.3−11, 8

Petronius
  Satyrica 65.3−9, 126
  85−87, 127
Philo
  De vita contemplativa 7.60−3, 121−23
Plato
  Apology 19c, 104
  23a−b, 87
  28c1−d4, 110
  Charmides 154d1−e6, 94
  Phaedo 58d5−6, 27
  60b−c, 66
  Phaedrus 228a−b, 29
  237b7−d4, 43−44
  Republic 3.403b5−c1, 49
  6.495b8−c6, 85
  9.573d1, 82 n.6
  Symposium 172a−3e, 20−29
  173b5−6, 28

Plato, *Symposium (continued)*
    174a3–d3, 29–33
    175b1–2, 32
    175d, 26, 33
    175e, 33
    176e4–5, 5 n.4
    177a3, 54
    177b5–6, 36
    177d2–3, 36
    177d5, 5
    178a5–80b9, 38–42
    179c1–2, 39
    179d4–5, 39
    180c–85c, 43–53
    180e4–81a6, 42
    184d3–e4, 106–7
    185a5–b5, 106–7
    185d1–e2, 54–55
    185e6–88e5, 53–59
    186c5–d1, 55–56
    188a–b, 66
    189a3–4, 60
    189b6–7, 60
    189d1, 60, 61
    189c2–93e3, 60–71
    191c6–7, 61
    191e7–92a1, 64–65
    192c3–d2, 68
    194e4–97e8, 71–77
    196d6–e6, 72–73
    197d1–e3, 73–74
    197e6–8, 74
    198c6–99a6, 36
    199b1, 78
    199b4–5, 36 n.36
    199c5–212c2, 24, 78–98
    200c–e, 80, 81
    201d3–5, 81
    201d5–e2, 24
    202e3–3a7, 84
    203b1–4a6, 85–87, 130–32
    203c6–7, 34
    204b1, 85 n.8

    204d–e, 87 n.12
    206c5–6, 88–89
    206d3–e1, 88
    209a8–c3, 90–91
    210e2–11d5, 95–97
    211c1, 93 n.21
    211d5–8, 83
    212b1, 99 n.27
    212b2, 97
    212c1–3, 36
    212d3–7, 98
    214a–b, 5
    215a5–22b7, 98–112
    215a6–b3, 100–101
    215e1–2, 101
    216e4–7, 10
    217a5, 26, 101
    218b–d, 14, 105–7, 129
    218b5, 14 n.16
    218d3, 90
    218e2–6, 107
    219a1, 105
    219a8–b2, 107–8
    220b7–8, 108
    220c3–d5, 32
    221c4–5, 110
    221e4–7, 10–12, 30
    222a7, 99 n.27
    222c1, 8
    223d, 19, 79
Plutarch
    Amatorius 762c, 103–4
    How to Study Poetry 10c–d, 13
    On Isis and Osiris 374c–e, 131–32

Xenophanes
    fr. 1, 6–7
Xenophon
    Memorabilia 1.2, 103–4
    1.2.29, 53
    Symposium 8.3, 40 n.2
    8.9, 45
    9.6, 16

General Index

Not every occurrence of the name of the principal speakers in the *Symposium* is recorded.

Achilles, 38, 39, 40, 41, 89, 110
Achilles Tatius, 18, 123, 127–28
Aeschylus, 39
Aesop, 65, 66
Agathon, 58, 71–81, 83, 84, 87 n.11, 109
   in comedy, 75–77
   poetic style of, 54, 75–77
Aischines of Sphettos, 81
Ajax, 109
Alcestis, 38, 39–40, 41, 89
Alcibiades, 4, 10–14, 42, 50, 51, 53,
      82, 90, 98–112, 114, 119–20, 126
Alexis, comic poet, 19–20
Allen, Woody, 119
Antisthenes, 11
Anytus, prosecutor of Socrates, 103
Aphrodite, 8, 10, 16, 44–47
   'Ourania', 44–47, 117
   'Pandemos', 44–47, 117
Apollo, 8, 57, 61, 62, 65

Apollodorus, 4, 20–29, 32, 82, 98,
      111, 114
Apuleius, *Metamorphoses*, 128–29
   On the God of Socrates, 130
Archelaos of Macedon, 4
Archilochus, 'Cologne Epode', 89
      n.16, 108 n.41
Ares, 8, 10
Ariadne, 13, 16
Aristippus of Cyrene, 46
Aristodemus, 4, 23–32, 82, 98, 111–12
Aristogeiton, Athenian hero, 52
Aristophanes, 53–54, 60–71, 84,
      117–19, 127
   Acharnians, 65, 70
   Birds, 64
   Clouds, 13, 52, 62, 66, 67, 92, 104
   Frogs, 92
   Knights, 61, 70
   Lysistrata, 66, 70

Aristophanes *(continued)*
  Peace, 60, 64, 70
  Wealth, 70, 85
  Women in Assembly, 70
  Women at the Thesmophoria, 58, 75–77
Aristotle, 15, 19
Asclepius, 57
Aspasia, 81–82
astronomy, 59
Athenaeus, 10, 31 n.33

Barthes, Roland, 113
Beauty, Form of, 19, 83, 96–97, 101, 106
beauty, stimulus to creativity, 91
Boeotia, 46
Brasidas, Spartan general, 110
Brecht, Bertolt, 109 n.43

Carpenter, Edward, 116, 117
Christ, Jesus, 12
Colorado, legal status of gay sex in, 125
Comedy, 30, 60, 61, 65, 79 n.1. *See
    also* s.v. Aristophanes
conversion to philosophy, 24–25
cooking, 58
Critias, Athenian politician, 53, 103

daimones, 84, 130
Delium, Athenian retreat at, 109
Delphic Oracle, 92
Demodocus, bard in Homer, 8, 10
Demosthenes, 19
Diogenes the Cynic, 11
Dionysus, 6, 13, 16, 18, 19, 33, 99, 100
Diotima, 9, 14, 19, 28, 31, 34, 57, 59,
    69, 70, 78, 81–98, 99, 100, 106,
    108, 129, 130–32
doctors, 33, 54, 61. *See also* s.v. Eryxi-
    machus; medicine

Elis, 46
encomium, 34–37, 56–17, 71
  rules for, 35, 71

Epictetus, 11
Epicurus, 15
epideixis ('display'), 28, 29–37, 54, 108
Er, myth of, 81, 97
Erasmus, 11–12
Eros/*erôs*, passim, esp. 15–20
Eryximachus, 14, 53–61, 66, 73, 81, 84
Euripides
  Hippolytus, 17–18
  Medea, 17
  Trojan Women, 17

Feuerbach, Anselm, 113
Ficino, Marsilio, *Commentary on Plato's
    Symposium*, 132–135
Forms, Platonic, 97. *See also* s.v.
    Beauty, Form of
Forster, E. M., 115–117
frames, narrative, 22–23
Freud, Sigmund, 118–119

Giants, 62
Glaucon, 23, 32
Gorgias, 33, 74–75, 101
  Encomium of Helen, 74
Great Dionysia, 3 n.1

Harmodius, Athenian hero, 52
Hedwig and the Angry Inch, rock-opera,
    67, 69 n.35, 119 n.11
Hephaestus, 8–9, 63–64, 68, 69
Heraclitus, 55
Hermes, 8
Herodotus, 14, 17
Hesiod, 38, 44–45, 65
hiccups, 55
Hippias, 38, 52
Hippocrates, Hippocratic corpus,
    55–56, 61
Homer, 8–10, 16, 31, 42, 109
homosexuality, female, 45. *See also* s.v.
    pederasty
hybris, 12, 13, 46

Ion of Chios, 14
irony, 11. *See also* s.v. Socrates

Lacan, Jacques, 117–120
Lenaian festival, 3 n.1
'likenesses', sympotic game, 5, 100–102
Lucian, *Symposium*, 22 n.20
Lucretius, 26
Lycurgus, Spartan lawgiver, 92
Lysias, 38, 39

Mantinea, 81
Marsyas, 101
medicine, 54, 55–56, 58
Menander, 19
Methodius, *Symposium*, 132
midwife, Socrates as, 90, 93
Murdoch, Iris, 126 n.24
musical theory, 56, 57–58
Mysteries, Eleusinian, 4, 14, 92–93
of *erôs*, 92, 99

Nestor, 110
novels, ancient, 68, 127–28

Odysseus, 102, 109–10, 127
Oedipus, 59
Orpheus, 38, 39

Pandora, 16, 65
parody, 9–10, 41, 54, 77
Patroclus, 39, 110
'Pausanian love', 116
Pausanias, 40, 42, 43–53, 56–57,
    68, 82, 89, 91, 94, 105, 106, 114,
    127
pederasty, Greek, 19, 43–53, 114–25,
    and passim
Peloponnesian War, 4
Penia ('Poverty'), 85, 100
Pericles, 110
    'Funeral Speech', 42, 114

Petronius, *Satyrica*, 126–27
Phaedrus, 14, 35–36, 38–42, 51, 52,
    80, 109, 110
philia, 16–17, 39–40, 48, 80, 91
Philo of Alexandria, 121–23
Pindar, 46 n.8, 72
Plato, passim. *See also* s.v. *Symposium*
    Apology, 37, 87, 92, 110
    Gorgias, 51, 71
    Laws, 58
    Menexenus, 82
    Meno, 89–90, 101–2
    Parmenides, 22, 23
    Phaedo, 3, 22, 27, 85, 89–90
    Phaedrus, 3, 19, 29, 33, 38, 39, 43–
        44, 50, 106, 115, 116, 135
    Protagoras, 41, 43, 52
    Republic, 3, 24, 27, 81, 97, 105 n.38
    Theaetetus, 22, 24, 90
Plotinus, 130–31
Plutarch, 15
    Amatorius, 46, 125–26
poetry, claims of opposed to philoso-
    phy, 31–32, 39, 110–11
Polemon, Platonic philosopher, 25
Polycrates, *Accusation of Socrates*, 103
Polymnia, Muse, 58
Poros ('Resource'), 85
Posner, R. A., judge, 120–21
pregnancy, psychic, 82–98, 100
Prodicus, 33, 43
Protagoras, 33, 52

Rabelais, 12
'recollection' (*anamnêsis*), 90
rhetoric, 34–37, 75
'*Rhetoric to Alexander*', 35
Rolfe, F. W. ('Baron Corvo'), 117
Rubens, 113

Sappho, 17
satyr drama, 99

Second Sophistic, 125
seercraft (*mantikê*), 56, 59, 81
Seneca, 26
Shelley, P. B., 123–124
Sicily, Athenian expedition to, 3, 4, 14, 17
Silenus, 6, 10, 11–12, 13, 70, 100–101
Sirens, the, 102
Socrates, passim
trial of, 4, 95, 104
Solon, 92
sophia, 72
sophists, the, 52
Sophocles, *Oedipus Rex*, 59
Trachiniae, 17
Sparta, 4, 110
speech, direct/indirect, 23–24
Speusippus, 15
Spice Girls, the, 69 n.35
spoudaiogeloion, 9–13, 36, 50, 98
Symposium (Plato), passim
date of, 3
dramatic date of, 4, 22

symposium, conduct of, 5–15, 34, 41, 81
in Homer, 8
literature of, 6–7, 19–20
of the Seven Sages, 15

Teiresias, 59 n.25
Testa, Pietro, 113
Theognis, 15, 18, 49
Thucydides, 42, 114
tragedy, Attic, 110–111. *See also* s.v. Agathon

'Uranians', 116

wine, 5, 18

Xenocrates, Platonic philosopher, 25
Xenophanes of Colophon, 6–7, 62
Xenophon, 103–4
Cyropaideia, 19
Symposium, 13, 15, 60

Zeus, 62, 63, 64